THE ALMIGHTY *and Me*

MY TESTIMONY OF RELIGION, REBELLION, AND RELATIONSHIP

KARL DANIEL GRABIN

The Almighty and Me

My Testimony of Religion, Rebellion, and Relationship

ISBN-13: 979-8662656-642

For we ourselves were also once foolish, disobedient, deceived, serving various lusts and pleasures, living in malice and envy, hateful and hating one another. But when the kindness and the love of God our Savior toward man appeared, not by works of righteousness which we have done, but according to His mercy He saved us, through the washing of regeneration and renewing of the Holy Spirit, whom He poured out on us abundantly through Jesus Christ our Savior, that having been justified by His grace we should become heirs according to the hope of eternal life.

(Titus 3:3-7)

THE ALMIGHTY AND ME

ACKNOWLEDGMENTS

To all the servants of the Almighty, diligently teaching His Word, and being an example. I am so grateful to sit at your feet and listen to the thousands of hours of sermons and teachings you have shared. Also, for all the times of personal Bible studies, prayers, and counseling with me. Blessings and peace to you all!

To my wife, Jacqueline, thank you for your support in all aspects of our life, you are a faithful helpmate. I love you so much!

To my children, thank you for encouraging me to write. Your patience and feedback made this book a reality!

To my parents, I'm forever grateful for your patience, kindness, and prayers. Your love for the Almighty and His Son is a light for so many!

THE ALMIGHTY AND ME

vi

TABLE OF CONTENTS

INTRODUCTION

Life is filled with choices, right from the Garden of Eden to the present day. Our decisions determine our religion, rebellion, or relationship, with the Almighty's creations and the Creator Himself.

The challenging time we live in has pushed me beyond my comfort zone to write this book. With so many people withdrawing from one another, it seems appropriate to share my struggles. How I've learned to be at peace with both the physical and mental challenges I face. I've learned to be thankful as I live and to use what the Almighty gave me to do what is right.

I realize others may have better stories than mine. Still, I hope that my small challenges will encourage others and possibly provide a method to help those experiencing horrific obstacles to overcome their own.

Spending the majority of time with immediate family can be an odd occurrence, which can no longer be ignored. I can genuinely say it is only by the Almighty's grace that I'm here today, thankful to be a husband and a father.

My testimony consists of events that paint the story of my life, brush after brush. I went from being a spectator in a congregation, to becoming a doer of the word of the Almighty. These events show the process of realizing the false worship I was caught in on and accepting responsibility for the choices I had made. Inviting the Almighty during the "battle," and finally believing and obeying His words. Some of these events can be described only as life-changing, supernatural, and a personal account that the Almighty exists. I will do my best to retell these snapshots. These memories are only a taste of the unadulterated reality.

I give you my story with anticipation that you will be encouraged to share your testimony of how the Almighty is working in your life. If you don't have a personal relationship with Him, my hope and prayer is that you will read this book and develop a partnership. Realizing how He has been in all our circumstances and learning to hear His voice in any situation. Finding guidance and healing from an unlimited source that wants to dwell within. He's here, right now!

LEAVING THE GARDEN

When I shut up heaven and there is no rain, or command the locusts to devour the land, or send pestilence among My people, if My people who are called by My name will humble themselves, and pray and seek My face, and turn from their wicked ways, then I will hear from heaven, and will forgive their sin and heal their land.

(2 Chronicles 7:13-14)

EARLY YEARS

I can still remember being lost in the woods with my family at four years old. My father was driving his 1981 Ford Granada on a country road in Colorado. It was late afternoon, and the heavily wooded forest was already getting dark. The sun had made its way to the western side of the mountains, and we all wondered if the next curve in the road would be the way back to the blacktop.

I was sitting on my mom's lap in the front seat, looking at the endless turns of steep winding roads. The grass was overgrown in the center where the car tires never touched. I could hear the blades of grass rubbing on the metal under the car.

When I wasn't looking out the window, I was looking at the eight-track player and wondered what it would be like to push even one of the buttons. I knew my dad would certainly scowl at the idea, and so, I did my best to behave.

Dad was a military man who loved the Almighty very much. He often took us on long drives, and we would visit different churches nearby. We attended our church regularly, and I could already pray like any spiritual adult would, believing to receive from the Creator, even at age four. Although Dad rarely got lost, this time was different. It seemed like a rancher closed a gate after we came through, and we were now scrambling to find another way out.

My confidence in my dad and the Almighty were unmovable. There was no doubt in my mind they could accomplish anything, even making us appear home in split seconds. So, when my dad asked us all to pray that we circle our way out of the woods before darkness fell, I knew exactly what to do.

The road was very steep, and the small car with five people was having difficulty keeping traction. Once we prayed, the situation was the same. Other members of the family were done with their prayers, but not me. I bowed fervently, and focused until we made it out; never once quitting, never once doubting.

Family and I

As a child, I thought my family was less privileged, but that was not the case. Most people lived within the town, in a neighborhood, but we lived about a ten-minute drive away. The house I grew up in was finished a few years before I was born. This place was my parent's dream home, sitting on eight acres. The dream home was backed up next to thousands of acres of open land; and allowed my brother, Timothy, and I many opportunities to explore. The driveway was a quarter of a mile long, the first half started flat and straight, and the second half curved up at a steep sixteen percent grade, toward the top of a hill. Our house was anything but ordinary; it sat on the hill with arresting views of the alfalfa field below, where cattle grazed, and the city in the distance. To the rear of the property were majestic scenes that went on for miles. The sights of mountains, rock formations, and juniper trees were so abundant. It was such a mesmerizing panorama.

At night, we would sometimes sit on the deck and look up at the stars and the distant city lights. While in the day, my brother and I would go hiking and search out and get familiar with the caves in the hills. We also built forts, collected fossils, and caught crawdads from the irrigation ditch. My sister, Christina, liked to pick fruits from the trees and would often study the wildlife. There were lots of birds, rabbits, chipmunks, deer, coyotes, and mountain lions.

My mother kept a large garden in the summer and made many tasty meals in the winter. My father, when he wasn't working, took pleasure in walking the property and irrigating the field. Life on our land was tranquil and relaxing, but I would often wish we could live in town. I wanted to play with more children and live closer to other people. The best way for me to meet people was when we went to church, and fortunately, my parents took us often.

At church, I still remember the long sermons that the preacher belted out for hours on end. As a little boy, I would find creative ways to keep myself entertained. Almost every Sunday, I would slowly melt in the pews until I finally made it to the floor. From there, I would low crawl as fast as I could until I could feel the pull of my mother's hand clasping firmly on my ankle. As she was sliding me back to my seat, I would try to grab other people's ankles, and would often snap an older lady's nylon sock along the way! The older ladies would jump up and yelp, as if a live serpent had curled around their calves. If you could have heard those ladies scream, you would understand why I frequented the parking lot of the church. The parking lot was my zone of instruction, where I received some energetic talk from my mother about respecting people's boundaries. Especially in the Almighty's house!

In elementary school, I had many friends. I always found ways to seek out someone hurting and encourage them. I would look for the person sitting alone in the cafeteria and invite them to my table of friends. The child being bullied during recess would also become my comrade, but I wouldn't stop there; I'd go after the bully. I took great pleasure in being judge, pronouncing the punishments of the bullies, and liberating those in need. My passion was kindled because I saw how people treated my friends less than human; it upset me.

Spending time with people suffering gave me a unique opportunity to see the consequences of people's ignorance and cruelty towards an innocent victim. Seeing this abundance of injustice at such a young age helped me understand that, not only the children in society were divided, but also the social systems of humanity.

The day after my eleventh birthday, we watched as the Berlin Wall was shown on Dad's rabbit-eared television. Those two antennas had to stay just right to get a clear picture. We had only four channels: five, eight, eleven, and thirteen, and each channel had to be tuned in just right to get the picture. My parents had their chairs, and the three of us children had ours on the floor, looking up at the ten-inch screen. The massive wall of South facing windows flooded the room with a glare on the TV by day, so we rarely watched it, but this day was special. The Berlin Wall was erected after World War II and divided the capital city of Germany into Eastern and Western sects.

Our attention was focused on the announcements as the division was coming down! A rush of euphoria and outburst of energy filled the atmosphere as people tore concrete structures to the ground with sledgehammers and cranes. This thick wall reminded me of the division in my own life between right and wrong, a boundary that should never be crossed. Somehow, I had become separated from the boy of faith who would continually pray until an issue came to pass, and was now trapped on the other side of the spiritual conscience. I wanted to tear my fortification down as they did on TV with such a force. I wanted to do the right thing each time, but the temptation of knowledge and pleasure kept pulling me deeper away.

My Early Adventures

Less than a year had passed, and my father was activated for Operation Desert Storm. I still remember how worried I was to say goodbye and watch him fade into the abyss. He would send me trading cards, much like a baseball card, but with photos of the different military crafts and their specifications. This new hobby was a soothing distraction as it placed my mind on pondering what was going on in the combat zone, thousands of miles from our hometown.

At school, the teacher would bring a television into the classroom on a wheeled cart, so during certain times of the day, we could watch what was happening during the conflict. I remember seeing this time as an opportunity to spend more time with friends. Often, I would push for a sleepover at their house and use the excuse that I missed my dad. I honestly did miss him, but I had become an opportunist. I was learning how to wage situations in life to work to my advantage.

As the years progressed, so did my ability to live a double life. I had spent time with the local church from birth until I left the house at age 19. My parents grew up going to church and had met at a church camp, so it was easy to have child-like faith in the Almighty's presence. On Sundays, we often attended services in the mornings and evenings. Wednesday nights, we would participate in Bible studies. During the Spring, Summer, and Fall, we would visit family camps, youth conventions, and vacation Bible school. The opportunities to learn the Almighty's ways and have His Son in my life were so frequent that I took them for granted. They meant little any longer, and I could easily forfeit them if I had my way.

I really thought that going to church and inviting friends was enough righteousness. Lots of times, I would bring a half dozen friends to church, and we would have a good time. It was all about food, games, and socialization. If given the opportunity, I would ask them if they had a personal relationship with the Almighty's Son and pray with them to accept Him into their lives. Many were willing, but just as I, we didn't really know what that meant. What were we to do after such a commitment? Why did we go on sinning just the same?

Science Over My Faith

Looking back now, I can honestly say that my spirituality was not as it seemed. I can see I had no personal relationship with the Almighty, like my parents or even I had expected. It was best defined as a social book club with catchy tunes. Or I was maybe learning how to fit in and say the right things at the correct times. This attitude is probably why in fourth grade, I stopped believing and evolved into someone who only trusted what I could see, touch, smell, and sense. I gave in to critical thinking that caused me to doubt the validity of my faith in the Almighty, the Bible, and even in myself. I was on a treacherous path that went from complete trust to investigating why things were right and wrong. I was learning through involvement and understanding, rather than through faith. Hence, my cravings for having new experiences skyrocketed.

Little did I realize that I had just made the same mistake our ancestors made nearly 6,000 years ago! I ate of The Tree of Knowledge of Good and Evil! I went from the child that would never touch a cigarette to stealing them from an uncle. From being modest to committing adultery in my heart! And the list goes on! Yes, at age ten, my life was changing while I just watched. My eyes were now opening, and I was also severely exposed. Many things my parents had protected me from were now those things I found enticing. Every time I had a minimal taste, I wanted more. As I had more, I felt guilty. My parents didn't smoke, yet here I was hiding this from them.

It didn't take long for remorse to broadly receive me with welcoming hands. The guilt was followed by lying to protect my appearance. I desired to say something but never did say anything because I was scared. I feared talking to someone else about my predicament. I feared anyone else knowing about my shameful adventures! I wanted to hide and cover myself, just as Adam and Eve did in the garden. My peace and innocence were more easily identified as a fading image in a rearview mirror. I was going down a superhighway to self-indulgence. My parents gave me hugs every night, but now I used the excuse I was getting too old. After all, I was the youngest, so it was easier to make it look like I wanted to be older like my siblings.

My friends also changed. I wanted to be around people who shared the same curiosity, who could give me access to the new experiences which I yearned for. My parents were very modest, and when I would ask if I could have a sleepover at a friend's, they would always say no. But persistence rose up, and I nagged and pushed for any chance to get out. At last, the door opened, and I spent the night away from home at a friend's house! Even then, I kept pushing until the door was wide open, and I could spend the night on most weekends, and eventually, some weekdays. Finally, while I was in high school, I snuck out and stayed out for hours, sometimes all night.

As silly as this may sound, one of the root motivators in my life was music. What started as singing praises slowly but intentionally let a little more of the world in, until my soul embraced it. Once the new idea or sound no longer seemed foreign, that marked the time a newer one became introduced. In elementary school, the songs allowed provocative thoughts to enter and caress my mind. It was as if when I'd hear the song again, I could see the video playing in my mind. And by high school, I was listening to music so wicked that I won't even mention the things I saw or heard. This addiction was a form of programming and was far from the reality I was taught.

Disaster in Our Home

One day during my sophomore year in high school, I was skipping school and joyriding with my friend. We had the music turned up and basked in the ecstasy of being free. To our surprise, my father pulled up behind us, flashing his truck lights, so we pulled over. As he approached us, my heart sank because I knew a lot of what I was hiding was likely to be exposed and dealt with at this moment. We already had the windows rolled down, so when he looked in and said, "Karl, go get in the truck!" I didn't hesitate. I remember seeing my mother sitting in the middle of the bench seat, looking straight ahead. I tried to pry her for information to see how much she knew of my deceitfulness and figure out an angle of approach.

My father was talking to my friend for a long time, and I was getting anxious. Finally, I looked at my mom and asked what was going on. She said my brother died. I couldn't believe this! He was home from college, and the night before, we argued. I remember my brother storming out and had thought nothing of him, but now I was feeling great remorse. My hardened heart briefly softened and caused me to feel regret. First, a blurred sight, then tears filled my eyes, then a stream rushed down my chin. I could not hold back. The brother I used to be best friends with was now absent in my life.

Hearing all of this, it seemed apparent my life was a different ball game. Still, sadly, the people I socialized with were indifferent. We were part of the "system," which is a product of uncensored life at a young age in small-town America. What appeared very safe was a deception. It would seem it all was just a phase. By the end of high school, I was an Eagle Scout (the highest achievement in Boy Scouts of America), played the drum set during church services, talented on the piano, and had dozens of friends. To top it all off, I received acceptance into an accredited Christian college and would now leave home.

Two weeks before graduating high school, I received a call at my workplace from my mom. She said our house was on fire and I had to come home right away. High winds had downed a power line into the stacked firewood behind the house. When I arrived at the scene, it was so surreal. Several fire trucks and workers diligently fighting to put out the flames. After several hours, all that remained were the stone walls and the foundation. It was shattering, and this moment was a symbolic representation of my own life. Much damage was done, but there was still a solid cornerstone left of the rubble to build back anew. If I was willing to burn off the unrighteousness in my own life, I could reconstruct the Biblical foundation drilled within my heart.

LATER YEARS

My College Days

Whew! I made it through high school, and that was not easy, either! But college was on the horizon. It was time to put "childish" things away.

With this new beginning, I thought to break off from the chain of challenges that had enslaved me since I was ten years old! I had attended a private Christian school for two years in elementary school. I was looking forward to the firmness of discipline to curtail me once more. Once I was in this controlled environment, I would be able to stay away from the addictions that now ruled my life, and live freely and at peace. I gripped onto this conviction like it was my eleventh-hour.

The first few days of college were tremendously stressful. I had to step out of my comfort zone and meet new people. Even living with a roommate in the dorms was like having my brother alive again. He seemed to always be in my space at the wrong times. I also had to leave my car with my parents for the first semester, which made it difficult to sneak away. I was trying to act like I wasn't going through any withdrawals. Still, the challenges of these new experiences were painful. If I could have sucked it up for a few more weeks, I would have been on the road to recovery, but wouldn't you know that trouble finds itself even when you are not looking?

In the first week, I met a foreign exchange student. He was friends with someone who had not only a car but also an apartment off-campus. He smoked and drank, and we'll leave it at that. Relieving myself with these habits helped, but once again, I was trapped. Only this time, it was caught in the flames of addiction, and I had to hide everything even more. It seemed like I had found my long-lost double life and had graduated to a college-level of lies and deceit. Once again, things looked great on the outside; I was in the school choir, band, attending a Bible college and even maintained a clean looking haircut this time. I felt like such a hypocrite!

Throughout my first year of college, I studied aviation, hoping to become a pilot for missionaries. During one of my solo flights, the weather took a quick change; the winds switched directions, and the sky was darkening up. I had checked the weather report before departing, but with such distressing weather, I was unclear about what to think. There wasn't supposed to be a storm right then. I truly believed it was a wakeup call from the Almighty to change my ways and restore me. I cried out to him to save me and re-plotted a course back home. Once I landed, it was as if nobody at the airport realized there was even a storm. This bizarre encounter seemed to tune up how foolish I thought I was, and sadly, within a few days, I had hardened my heart again.

My Transfer to a State School

After I completed two years of exceptional education and mentorship, I received an associate degree. I then transferred to a State school. Finally, no more dual personality and lying about who I am, it was absolutely time to be transparent.

The University of Colorado was a fun fit after being stuffed up in a place where I had to lie to be accepted. Contrary to my beliefs, now, I could openly do things I had been doing over a decade in private, and it was the norm. You would think this would solve the problem, but no! Problems find the troubled heart. I wanted to scrub the religion and lies off to start again.

After I transferred, my dad talked me into applying for an Army Reserve Officer Training Corps (ROTC) scholarship. I couldn't have blamed him, as two years of paying tuition for a private college is very expensive. Within my first week, one of the ROTC Cadre had approached me to start up a Bible study, and I couldn't say no.

Looking back, I realized that I went to church on Sundays. I longed for the moments of praising and fellowshipping with other Believers. Meanwhile, momentarily, I was living a double life and about to have a college degree in lukewarm double-faced hypocrisy at its finest. I even received a leadership award for being an "example" for others to follow. When a prayer was in order, I knew just what to say and how to say it. Inside, my life was fading away. I didn't even care anymore. One day I'm praising the Almighty, and the next, I'm at a bar talking wicked.

I thought that was the end of my internal conflicts, but it was all lies. Another destructive addiction forming in my life was gambling. As a child, we played lots of card games, like canasta during family gatherings and poker on camping trips. Now, I was 22 years old and could go to the casinos. Almost as soon as I started going, I became a regular. I would bring a few hundred dollars and play all day. Often, I did well enough that the casino comped me food and a room for the night.

This hospitality only tipped me to play more—a whole lot more! Often, it was like a roller coaster, up one minute and down the next. I would sit there, smoke, drink, and watch my money slowly trickle away. If I made money, I would save it for the next game to keep the habit going. Gambling had me in shackles and chains. I rarely walked away with anything other than disappointment and a desire to play more and earn more.

One of the best ways for me to relieve stress was running. As a cadet, we did plenty of running in the mornings, but I would often go for a five to ten mile run in the mountain trails on the weekends. At one point, we trained and did a marathon in White Sands, New Mexico. The race was in memory of the prisoners of war from the Bataan Death March of 1942. The event was done in full combat gear, rucksack, and rifle throughout various terrain, and ended in miles of thick loose sand that was so exhausting. The best part of the finish was actual survivors of the original march shook our hands as we crossed the finished line. I did not place first, but staying stride for stride with Navy Seals and Green Berets running the course gave me all the motivation I needed.

Another sport I did was cycling. Mostly during the warmer months, I would do century rides (100 miles) throughout the mountain highways and plains. My father and I even had the pleasure of doing an event called "Ride the Rockies." Every year the Denver Post newspaper would host a week-long cycling event. A select number of people were picked to ride through the mountain highways in a race-style event that felt a little like the Tour de France. We rode for over four-hundred miles that week and negotiated a different mountain pass every day. We even saw our family doctor there and rode with him most of the week too! This was one of the most beautiful memories I had during these healthy times of my life.

I really felt connected with the outdoors and loved to take in the mountains and nature. Often, I would head to Breckenridge to ski during the winter and would backpack a lot in the summer. I usually did these events alone as my solitude with the Almighty's creations soothed my soul. Sometimes I would go backpacking and be gone for a few days. One of the most memorable moments was when I had driven several hours to hike a fourteener, a mountain that's

14,000 feet above sea level. I had planned to start early that morning and set up camp but was delayed. Once I reached the trail, it was already afternoon, and the weather quickly changed. I immediately thought about my experience in the airplane and the infamous storm. Was the Almighty going to show me His glory again? Suddenly, huge flashes of light filled the darkened sky and heavy down pouring rain. I was already over 13,000 feet, and there was hardly any vegetation. I thought about how I shouldn't be up at this height in the afternoon because of storms like this but was so determined I ignored common sense and pressed forward.

After about twenty minutes, the sky looked like night, and the thunder shook the earth like artillery rounds exploding. I remember seeing a herd of elk with a big bull looking up at me. He was so calm and collected. Could it be I imagined this event? Hardly! I was feeling so out of place, I turned and ran back to my car. As beautiful as this was, I was terrified. My breath kept a steady pace as I sang military cadence quietly. Round after round exploding near enough to wonder how I was still standing. I cried out to the Almighty and asked Him to save me again. I wanted to be safe and turn to Him. Once I made it back to the car and lower elevation, I looked up at the cloud-covered mountain and was grateful to be alive!

About a year later, one of the most memorable moments in modern history occurred. It was September 11, 2001. After physical training (PT) with the other cadets, I finished my morning routine of showering and breakfast. When I went to class, the cadre announced what had happened.

These Twin Tower buildings in New York City were the same ones I visited during my days in Boy Scouts. I still remember laying on the sidewalk looking up to take a picture, because, on top, a platform prevented us from seeing straight down. Now, at this time, they were both leveled to the ground. The war on terrorism would rapidly be breaking out. Soon I would be finished with my schooling and be marching out to war.

I could bet even the guidance counselor in high school, who thought I wouldn't amount to anything, would have been shocked! I was beginning to seem successful! I had received many scholarships, grants, and was in great shape. I graduated top of my class in ROTC and also earned the George C. Marshall Award. I could pretty much pick any job and location I wanted after I got commissioned as an Army Officer. This guaranteed a great start after graduating from college!

Going to War

Military life was very natural. I had spent a lot of time in front of people, and the language and parties were so exciting! Much of my time and money was spent on things that made me feel "good" and significant. And unlike the college life, no one was approaching me to live a double life, nor my conscience wearing a court wig and rubbing my wrong dealings to my face. I had graduated into completely being in the world and of the world. Time was racing quickly, and one unrighteous choice after another was feeding the buildup of guilt and anger. I did not realize the spiritual sickness eating me up until depression had taken root inside of me.

So now, I had officially given up my core values, which my parents indoctrinated as a child. I gave up those echoed in Sunday school. My life was multi-faced, leaving off a flawless façade, and I didn't even see I was failing. Sometimes I would pray and thank the Almighty for something or when I needed some help, but after a few years, even that faded till I lost my communion.

A few years had passed, and my unit was activated as first responders for Hurricane Katrina. During this time, I was a communications Platoon Leader. We had to be ready to deploy anywhere in the world and set up voice and data for the commanding generals. This service allowed the leaders to communicate with subordinates and with the president. I'll never forget the challenges we faced traveling there: downed trees in the roads, flooding, and high winds. Hurricane Wilma also came shortly after and kept interfering with our satellite dishes and antennas, causing the signals to drop frequently. I never imagined the missions to be this challenging during training, as I wanted to be a reliable source for others to do their jobs and communicate properly.

I would chat at a minimal, pausing, stuttering, heaving, and then completely give up talking with others. Times of confidence was lessoning, and in 2006 I was diagnosed with major depressive disorder. Doing simple things like getting out of bed, or taking a shower, proved arduous to achieve. I would have to force myself to do what used to be a routine task. Even eating and sleeping were almost nonexistent. It wasn't until after a year in a combat environment, during Operation Iraqi Freedom, that I would reach a new low. A low that ultimately led me to where I am today. A low that pose as last straw to break.

I cried out to the Almighty and said that once I'm retired from my career, I would take time to read His word, The Bible, all over. Cover to cover, every word, and every letter. I'll study and know what it means! I was serious because I could not stand who I was becoming. Such habits helped me to escape my reality, and the guilt of it wasn't working anymore. I had become so low I hardly cared for myself. Well, you can imagine an Army captain, unkempt, quiet, reserved, and soft-spoken. I would do the minimum to get by and just try to stay alive. I felt terrible for the people around me because it must have been very uncomfortable to be around someone nice, but uninterested in every activity.

Just within a few weeks after I said that prayer, an explosion had caused me a great deal of discomfort. There were lots of explosions going off all the time, but this had knocked me down and rung my bell. I had a ringing in my ears that just wouldn't go away. What seemed like just another scary incident turned out to be one that later lead to a further medical investigation.

During this same time, one colleague was kind and brave enough to get to know me. Jacqueline was an intelligence officer, and when she wasn't busy would often come by my office and see how I was doing. Often, she would bring me orange juice and a muffin from the mess hall. I had no appetite but would eat it to show gratitude. I thought she was only doing this because I helped her get transferred from another location, but she kept coming back. Day after day, she would stop by and see if I wanted to go to the gym and work out. I felt so obligated to my work, but I knew I needed to stay in shape.

We started running together in the mornings and having dinner together in the evenings. If I knew no better, this was seeming like a date! I was grateful for her attention but was dating someone else back in the United States at the time and just enjoyed her company. After a while, I opened up to her about how frustrated I was with my life. She mostly listened and continued to stay by my side.

It's hard to imagine combat being beautiful. Still, Al-Faw Palace was one of the many residences of Former Saddam Hussein. This fortress was now the headquarters for the Multi-National Force-Iraq, and our unit was attached in support for them. Jacqueline and I would often walk along the mote and feed the geese and fish. Such a relaxing moment in such a stressful time.

After a few months, I stopped dating the girl back in the States. My desires for her went down and for Jacqueline up. As with many, being away for nearly a year, it's easy to grow apart when there's no commitment. Now it really was a date! But we had to behave ourselves as this was a real-world mission, and we needed to stay focused.

Seemed like every day, there were explosions, rocket attacks, and the occasional small arms rounds zipping by. On Thanksgiving night in 2007, it was no different. Jacqueline and I were in a hardened building because it was too dangerous at the time. I really wanted to propose to her outside under the moonlight near the water. Still, the desire was so intense I would not wait any longer! I asked, and she said, "Yes!"

A few days passed, and another colleague called me up and was trying to give me a hard time. She heard I was sharing muffins with Jacqueline, but when I told her she had the old news, I'm sure whoever got to see her face had a good laugh. I told her Jacqueline is now sporting a one-carat diamond, and we plan to marry as soon as we return to the United States!

We finished that deployment about six months after the explosion incident. I strut with much pomp as I left – it was all false. I was too ashamed to admit that I wasn't thinking correctly. Sometimes, I would even forget what was going on and what I had recently said. Battalion meetings were embarrassing, as I had lost most of my confidence to speak, the line of thinking and retrieving memories was painful to process. I also became clumsy and stumbled a lot. Sadly, I wasn't drinking or eating anything, and this was just the new norm.

Once I returned to the United States, I took about a month off. In the first week, I made an appointment with a neurologist. I was hoping to find out some answers about my deteriorating health. When I went to the doctor, I explained my situation, and he was sure it was nothing, but because I was so sincere, he ran some tests. I guess it seemed rather strange to wait for months to get some help, but for a person that was so depressed, even getting out of bed and taking a shower was a struggle. This doctor's visit required a great deal of courage as it caused me to humble myself and to admit something was wrong.

One test the doctor ordered was a magnetic resonance imaging (MRI) of my brain. I went in early one morning, and once the scanning started, the one person in the room stopped scanning for a long time. Then, I could hear quite a few people entering the room, and they asked me questions about why I had the scan. I shared with them a little about the explosion and how things were becoming more challenging to process. I asked if everything was okay, and they said the doctor would talk to me once the test was complete. They continued running the scans, and when they were finished, I was sent out of the room. Upon exiting, I noticed several doctors were looking hopelessly at my scans. They stopped momentarily and looked at me as if they had great pity and concern, and then went back to analyzing.

I must have waited a few days and got tired, so I resumed work. One day, the neurologist called me and left a message to call him back right away. I was terrified because a few months had passed now, and I knew something was wrong on my inside, but I didn't know what to expect from the doctor. I called him back right away, and he answered, which made me more concerned as most doctors will let the call go to voicemail and call back at their convenience. He told me to come in and see him the next day and that he would go over my test results. When I met up with the doctor, he explained my report from the radiologist. He said there were multiple lesions on my brain, and the complaints I had made corresponded with them. This news was a huge relief! Finally, someone recognized my condition. It wasn't just a figment of my imagination! I had a complaint, and now a valid physical match revealed with the MRI scan. I sighed.

Unfortunately, what followed shattered me. The doctor said, "Even though it looks like you have multiple sclerosis (MS), it probably isn't anything." I couldn't believe it! Just as I was about to have a diagnosis for this issue, it felt downplayed into nothing. He said he'd run more tests, but he didn't think I had MS.

My Retirement

During the next two years, the Army put me on a temporary retirement because of my health issues. I spent many hours going through various therapies to help improve my mobility and cognitive health. This was very awkward because I was aware of what was going on but would often blank out in mid-sentence and have incomplete thoughts. Speech pathology a few times a week, psychiatry and psychology a few times a month, and neurology every few months. These were the essentials of the healing process. I learned that one of the most important ingredients to a healthy brain was to eliminate stress. Before I would run marathons or ride centuries on my bike, but now I had to learn to cope in new ways.

Fortunately, the Almighty gave me a real helpmate. Jacqueline was more a "Believer" than most I have ever known. Her actions gave me hope and reason to try every day. Almost one year from the time we started dating, we were married on the summer solstice. I wanted it to be the brightest day of the year, as Jacqueline indeed was like the warm sunshine to me.

Interestingly, precisely one year from proposing to her, Jacqueline went into labor, and we had our first son, Timothy! The labor lasted twenty-two hours, and our almost nine-pound baby was born! Excitement quickly turned to fear as they took Timothy from the room to the intensive care unit.

I had to make a quick choice, stay with my exhausted wife, or follow our newborn. I knew Jacqueline would want me to stay with our young son, so off we went. His oxygen levels were deficient as he had fluid in his lungs. Lots of poking and prodding while trying to stay calm. Not quite the vision of passing a box of cigars to my fellow mates as I shout, "It's a boy!" Instead, I was in this new reality.

This experience was almost as challenging as trying to convince the doctor we wanted Timothy to be circumcised. One of the doctors kept telling us there was no need to do this because it was no longer a hygiene issue. Even though I told him it's a Biblical thing, it wasn't until he heard our family had done this for generations, he finally backed off. It seemed as if it was such a strange issue to wrestle with.

Once Jacqueline went back to work, we had decided since I was on sabbatical, I could watch Timothy while she was at work. If you could imagine, a forgetful stay at home dad trying to please his obsessively clean wife was quite the undertaking. I had checklists like I was doing a layout before a mission. I armed myself with a bottle of sanitizer, pre-pumped breast milk, and a diaper bag. Meanwhile, I was now walking with a quad-cane for more stability. The physical therapy was becoming too painful, so I spent more time sleeping between doctors' visits.

My father offered to come out and help since he was retired. It was quite a sight to see my early-sixties father changing diapers and cooking. If he hadn't shown up, I probably would have stopped going to the doctors, and who knows where that could have led?

About this time, Jacqueline's unit was preparing for a deployment to Iraq. They were doing training in different states, so breastfeeding became a very emotional experience. She was so sincere that she pumped ahead and froze quite a bit. She was even going to the extreme of overnight mailing the milk on dry ice from her training areas.

You should have seen us; we called ourselves Mr. Grandma and Mr. Mom! My dad stuck around for several weeks at a time, but eventually, he convinced me to put Timothy in daycare. This was a huge concern as he was sick for several weeks after he was born. My earthly father was right, though, I needed help, and I had to humble myself and ask.

Within the first week, Timothy ended up sick at home, and I missed quite a few doctor's appointments. I figured it was just a new environment, and he needed to build up some immunity. After a few days, Timothy was well enough to try going back. This went on for several weeks until finally, he ended up in the hospital. He had pneumonia again and was back on the machines for a few days. Such a heartbreaking experience to see him so helpless. My own issues were non-existent. There was no way I would let this happen again, especially with my wife away in a combat zone!

I let one of the providers at the childcare center know I was pulling Timothy out, and she completely understood. To my surprise, she called me up a few hours later to ask if I would be interested in hiring her for in-home care. This was bold! How could I have another woman in my home while my wife was gone? On the other hand, how could I keep giving mediocre care to my son? I needed to get back to my treatments, as well. Surprisingly, my wife was very much for this help as she was equally concerned for both of our health. What a blessing! Timothy now had someone to provide the care he needed, which meant I could focus on healing.

About this point in my life, I was diagnosed with MS. The excellent treatment for the rebuilding of my memory and other therapies had put me in a more stable situation. At the end of those two years, everything was finalized, and the Army awarded me a retirement with full benefits! It was such a blessing to be relieved of the stress of figuring out how to make a living while coping with the new physical realities. This blessing also allowed for me to have time with my new family.

I was now spending less time in the hospital and more time with my wife and son. Watching him grow so fast had been quite an experience I had desperately wanted to avoid. Mainly because getting married and having children were commitments that must be taken seriously. I didn't want to be a disappointment to my family or worse a hypocrite! It was time to hold onto my word, to step it up now. For righteousness sake, I was a husband and a father!

My prayer from over two years ago was now being fulfilled. I was retired and bestowed all the time to read my Bible! This came as not just what I had in mind, but the Almighty knew I was serious about studying His word and learning the truth about life. Therefore, it was time to start, but where do I begin?

TEST ALL THINGS

Test all things; hold fast what is good.

(1 Thessalonians 5:21)

Hours and hours unrestricted that I could read my Bible, seeking the Almighty and finding His truth. The only obstacle holding me back was my health, which, in reality, was ironically the only obstacle allowing me this plenteous time. It was awkward to have a disease that no one could see but filled my body with pain; and to look like a young, healthy, thirty-year-old man staying home while his wife went to work. Since then, I've learned to be careful of my words as I have learned from the Bible, we can speak healing or more sickness just by opening our mouths.

A Beckon

Jacqueline and I met in Georgia, but she was now being transferred to a new duty station in Hawaii. Although she was born in the Philippines, most of her life was spent on Oahu. Her parents were still living on the island, and it seemed we would now have more time to get to know one another better.

Her father, Jeffrey, was retired from the United States Navy, and we had many great conversations together. Her mother, Esperanza, worked as a cashier at the Pearl Harbor Commissary, and made delicious cuisines from her home country! I was feeling like a part of the family, but I missed my parents and sister back in Colorado.

I took a trip back with my son, Timothy, to visit my parents because my wife was deployed again to Iraq. While visiting, I noticed a church about a half a block from my parents' house. Never thought much of it before, but there was a calling in my spirit that said, "Go, check it out and see what you can learn." The few weeks of visiting my parents turned into a one-on-one Bible study with the pastor of the church. I learned so much during the time, it was incredible!

It drives me to tears to think that during the studies, "Was I learning something new? Or was it something I had forgotten and was re-learning in the Bible?" Maybe the Almighty knew I had created so many bad memories I would need to have my brain erased. Most likely, I both learned stuff afresh and re-learned such as I acquired as a child. I still have many memories, and probably didn't take my Bible studies as a child very seriously. But as soon as I returned to Hawaii, I attended a church and got involved with reading the Bible on my own.

I Lost My Son

During that year, my wife and I were expecting another child. The pregnancy was going well until one day I received a phone call from a paramedic. Jacqueline was in an ambulance and on the way to the hospital. In a bounce, I left home, and in another, I met her where she was and didn't know what to expect. The doctor said she was bleeding, and we could have our baby early.

The hospital's policy was that our baby was too young to put on life support and would most likely die. Jacqueline laid weak on the hospital bed, where her whole body was inverted to delay the labor. A week later, William Nathaniel Grabin was born. I still remember his little hand clenching my index finger as he looked up at me. He gasped for air, and the tears that dripped off my chin splashed on his forehead. His moment of death was one of the saddest and most helpless I've ever felt. I was angry and needed some peace and understanding in my life.

I Lost My Faith

A few weeks later, someone knocked on the door and asked if I would like to study the Bible with them. This encounter was perfect timing and was not a coincidence because I needed to be discipled.

For the next eighteen months, I studied the Bible with this man. I also did individual studies and even researched with many different other Believers. Some things I learned shocked me, while other things made me feel anger. Many things gave me great peace and hope for the life to come. Now, this is what I was hoping to find. Peace. True peace, detached from religion, and to have a genuine relationship with the Almighty Himself!

Learning something, I would apply these concepts in my life. Some were so foreign that it felt awkward and even caused tension with family and friends. Sadly, such open searching led to a devastating fork in the road. I had encountered some sincere individuals who no longer trusted the validity of the Apostle Paul's letters. As a student of truth, I openly listened, but without the Word of the Almighty planted deep in me, it was easy to be misled and believe their studies. This caused me to not only doubt Paul's letters, but also Peter's epistles. Eventually, I even lost trust in

Luke's writings and trickled down to eliminating all the gospel books.

My searching was creeping into other religions. What started as understanding the Bible was now leaning towards studying other books that opposed my very upbringing. How did I get to this point? One little change after another, I was being deceived. Fortunately, a Believer took time to educate me on how I was being misled and was able to pull back towards the Bible. But I had my doubts about all the religious writings. Were they truly inspired by the Almighty, or was this all created by man to control people?

Unfortunately, I also concluded where I either needed to step into more belief and act on it or back off and return to the life that seemed sensible. I wanted to keep the peace around the house. After all, we wouldn't want to be in some cult or teach our children things so different than the world we knew. I was scared, and for the next six years, I left my search for truth with the Almighty and returned to the world.

SIX YEARS OF RUNNING

And these are the ones by the wayside where the word is sown. When they hear, Satan comes immediately and takes away the word that was sown in their hearts. These likewise are the ones sown on stony ground who, when they hear the word, immediately receive it with gladness; and they have no root in themselves, and so endure only for a time. Afterward, when tribulation or persecution arises for the word's sake, immediately they stumble.

(Mark 4:15-17)

Since I didn't know who knew the truth, I gave up my research. All the stress of the unknown answers was driving me towards insanity. I gave more time to my family. We simplified our lives and tried our best to keep peace and order. I thought things would be different since I was married, but the opposite played out. Often, I used my disease as an excuse to be less involved with family life. I would take my medicine and sleep most of the days and nights.

Surprisingly, now that I left off the stress of religion and my rigorous pursuit of truth altogether, my life was even more hazardous than before. I had no guide, nor a signal of direction on what next to do. I surrendered to being guided by my feelings! This decision was dangerous! I would do nothing unless I felt like it. I had become a giant child for my wife to take care of, and now with our daughter, Chloe, born, we had even more responsibility.

Adventures with Jacqueline

During this time, Jacqueline finished out her twelfth year in the Army and resigned. So many challenges with child care, combat deployments, and my health it made more sense to live simple. We liquidated all our properties and assets and moved to a location that was beautiful yet affordable. There, in Post Falls, Idaho, we built our dream home and stayed in it for only a short while. We had so many rooms, and so much space, it felt like a marathon passing through from one corner to the other. Most of the time, we only used about three rooms. Soon, we felt overwhelmed by the space.

In less than a year, we sold the dream home and bought a recreation vehicle (RV). I wanted to be on the go, as my mobility was limited, and I didn't know what the future held. I wanted to make some memories with my family while we were young and available to each other. Our goal was to travel the mainland of the United States and see as many national parks as possible. My wife spent most of her life living on islands, so this would be a great time to show her the rest of the country. Also, our children were young enough; they wouldn't need to attend elementary school for a few more years. So, we liquidated everything again and went on an adventure of a lifetime!

Over three years, we went from coast to coast, visiting, and living in locations, long enough to enjoy them, and then move on to the next desired destination. We lived quite simple and often saved money by staying in RV parks on the military bases. I felt like a sojourner, like Abraham, but was more like Jonah because I was running from my responsibilities ushered by the Almighty's word; for me to share with and teach my family. Little by little, my addictions continued increasing, and the façade remained that I was doing "fine."

Often, I would park somewhere the family enjoyed and look for the nearest casino. I thought if they were in a desirable spot, they wouldn't mind if I did my own thing. I would often come home and give them a few hundred dollars of the winnings and assume that would suffice for my absence. Most of the time, it did; but sometimes I would come home with the answer, "I lost a few hundred dollars," and my absence was now a sour event. They wanted my time, not my money.

Eventually, running in the RV wasn't enough. Just as the other addictions failed to save me, so did the traveling. Instead of turning to the Almighty, I took up sailing. The lack of stress in my life had helped me to heal enough physically. I thought, "why not take it to the next level?" After discussing the idea with Jacqueline, she was willing to do this as a family, as long as I properly learned what to do.

For one year, I went to a sailing school and learned the basics and how to deal with heavy weather. A lot of the process reminded me of my aviation days. Mentally this was a very healthy move that gave me some positive way to express myself, but physically it was very exhausting. My body might have been mid-thirties in appearance, but it felt as if I were in my late sixties in pain and mobility. But I persevered and bought a small sailboat.

If you think living in a motor home is cramped, do not try to live aboard a sailboat! My wife was now homeschooling Timothy. Chloe and I would walk up the dock and find a playground. The children wore lifejackets down below, and I would tether them to the jack lines on deck.

We planned to circumnavigate the globe over the next ten years. A lot of me was missing all the backpacking, cycling, and running I used to do, so this became my new marathon. We spent several weeks in San Diego, California, preparing and training for the voyage. Eventually, we set sail and headed south.

Something I quickly realized was that day sailing was hard enough, although I could rest for a few days after and be okay. The 'passage maker' stuff was more than my body could handle. We took twelve hours to reach Ensenada, Mexico, and I knew that for the safety of the family, we needed to stay for a week and rest. Jacqueline and the autopilot helped a great deal. Still, the stress and fatigue of sitting up and being alert were beyond measure.

We stayed there for a month. Every time we were about to leave, something in my spirit said, "Stop!" This was hard to take because most of my pride was gone already, and I wanted some sense of accomplishment. I wanted to do something huge! After a few more day trips, I humbled myself, and we left the boat there till a later date.

My parents came out and joined us one time, and we went to Catalina Island for a week. We stayed either on anchor or moorings and would take the dinghy onto the land. It was a great adventure, but with my health, it was a poor choice to continue this lifestyle. As they said in sailing school, "Sailing is a young man's sport." So we sold the boat.

My attempts to run afar like Jonah were now back on land, and the RV adventures continued on. When my oldest child, Timothy, was a first-grader, he was accepted into an excellent charter school. Many people applied to this school, but they only had so many spots available. We had put him on the waiting list when he was born, in hopes to get in. Our current location was in Buffalo, NY, on our way to Newfoundland. Still, when we heard he was accepted, we abandoned the adventures and headed to my hometown. Once there, we bought a small house and began a new segment in life.

I didn't like who I was becoming, a person that knew there were huge duties but had run from taking responsibilities. I also didn't like the thoughts that came to me having learned the truth about the Almighty's ways. I was ignoring them because they were uncomfortable. The things I had learned about the Bible went against much of the doctrines and traditions I practiced, and they required undivided devotion to the Almighty. He gave me this time off to get to know Him, not to sit around and feel sorry for myself. It seemed I scurried my way up to The Tree of Knowledge of Good and Evil all over again. So here I was, seeing an opportunity to choose life, but I ignored it. I often thought about where I had left off on my search for truth. I didn't want religion; I wanted a relationship with The Creator and a way of living that led to life.

Using a Smaller Home

After selling the RV and settling into our new home, I took up painting. I was still suffering much physically and mentally on the inside, and art allowed me to escape to a new place every day. I had never done this seriously but had always desired to learn. We dedicated the back room of the house to my studio, and I created beautiful works. Soon, what planted as a seed to pass the short term, grew and became a way of sharing my new passion with others. This was my way to show what I longed for, exceedingly. I painted pictures of a perfect earth, skies, and serene. When I finished a particular work, I would share it with others on social media. Often, people would purchase my art, and this allowed me to buy more supplies, take more classes, and repeat the process.

My family seemed typical on the outside. We spent time in my hometown, and the children were accepted into an excellent charter school. They both were doing well in their classes and extracurricular activities. Over these years, I realized that I slipped back into heavy smoking and drinking. The Almighty had withered in my thoughts, speech, and actions. But The Creator, in His mercy, found ways to knock on the door of my heart, a knock I couldn't ignore.

Riding along with the tides of time, we came to meet with an unexpected event. My son Timothy would often get anxious at bedtime. I would try to assure him there's nothing to fear at night. He was safe, but that wasn't good enough, he wanted more; and after I was all out of ideas, I could only go back to praying to the Almighty. To my surprise, this worked! The Almighty Himself heard my prayers, and my son wasn't scared the rest of the evening. These undesired episodes went on for several years and would frustrate me. I didn't want to go down that road of having a relationship. I already knew too much, and it would require me to change and distance myself from the people I cared about.

The Almighty also used my daughter to speak to me. She would go out to the porch where I was smoking and drinking, and she would just hang around. I would do everything I could to convince her to go back inside the house and leave me alone. I told her, "You shouldn't be around me, I want to be left alone, I don't feel good, and you are too high energy." But none of these tactics worked on her.

The Almighty designed Chloe to love me unconditionally, and it was softening my stony heart. Often, she would bring me a breakfast tray loaded with fruits and vegetables. I would usually put my cigarette out for a bit and spend time with her, and she would make me laugh, and I would forget that I was sick and in pain. One time she even went so far to ask for me to quit smoking. It was her fourth birthday, and she wanted nothing else. I gave it a strong effort, but the desires to care were too weak.

My wife was also used by the Almighty to show me his power. There were so many times I was physically at home, but I traveled farther away across the earth. I find solace in escaping to be in a meadow, my parent's house, at my former deployment camp, yet never moving, never stepping from my couch. I would often spend the whole day on the porch drinking coffee in the morning and then switching to alcohol shortly after. She would call me to dinner, and I'd say, "No, thanks." She'd say it's time for bed, and I'd say, "No, thanks." She'd invite me to go to church with my parents, and I'd say, "No, thanks." If there was some work to do that I slipped from, I would have regarded myself as a couched potato. But I could barely do any work, and even when she invited me to do some pleasurable stuff, I wouldn't budge. I was more like our dog Oliver than a person, sitting on the porch half the day and using the other half on the couch.

Social Media

The stimulus of drinking and smoking were helpful distractions, but I wanted more to take away the pain. With smartphones and tablets readily available, I watched more movies and even played video games. For someone who liked running marathons and other extreme sports, this was about all my body was able to handle. I would virtually escape to go hunting, fishing, fighting, and racing, all from my front porch! These new apps on my phone made it easier than ever!

Our neighbors across the street used to think I was reading eBooks and was very academic until they spent time with me. They were both retired Army and would encourage me to keep painting. Often, they would come over and help by dumping my ashtray and empty bottles. At first, they thought the mess was from several days of neglect, but quickly learned it was from only a few hours. Their love and sense of humor often brightened my day. We would light up the front porch when the Denver Broncos won a game and sit and reminisce of our adventures in the military.

Another neighbor next door used to encourage me to paint by critiquing my work. She was in her late 80's at the time and had won many awards from her artwork. Chloe would frequently check on her to see if she needed anything and would often come back with a big smile and a candy bar. The neighbor's daughter became friends with us, and we kept her informed of her mother's well-being and health over those years.

It used to be very simple for me to socialize in person, but now I was doing this the easy way. Thinking I was being social, I would post some cute smiles with family, an adventure to the outdoors, a painting I just finished, or an interesting quote. All of these posts were my way to feel connected with others. What was happening, though, I was getting addicted to people liking what I shared and believed I was doing something productive. This went on for almost two years until I realized the "likes" from others wasn't making me feel happy anymore.

A good friend since the fourth grade would often come to visit. It was so refreshing to catch up and talk about baseball and television shows. He'd often come in the afternoon and spend most of the day with my family and me. Since I knew my friend, he was a huge Chicago Cub's fan and told me about this curse a man had put on the team. The man was the owner of a pet goat that was asked to leave due to its smells. So, from 1945, it seemed impossible for them to overcome and win the World Series. That year, 2016, the Cubs won the World Series, something neither of us thought we'd witness in our lifetime!

I realized while he was there, I could hardly look away from my electronic device long enough to stay engaged with him. My social skills and health often led me to lie down on the couch and just listen to him. It took so much energy for me to actually interact with another person that I often would fall asleep. Twenty-minute visits I could handle, but real intimacy was overwhelming. He'd stay for dinner, and this forced me to eat with my family. I enjoyed the time, but physically and emotionally, this was overwhelming.

Life was starting to downswing again. Only this time, I felt hopeless. I wanted to put an end to my life. On the other hand, I wanted to live, but that way seemed impossible. As long as I could be left alone, and distracted, I wouldn't have to deal with my reality, it hurt too much. I had so much anger and disappointment, I didn't even feel worthy of having a family. Many times, I felt like an institution would be a better fit. At least there, I could be sedated and just let the years pass by. But the thought of my children growing older without their dad, and my wife without her husband, crushed me deeply. I needed help, serious help. I was crying inside while looking withdrawn on the outside. I finally worked up enough courage to ask my wife if she would be willing to move. I needed change, and the habits I had formed were binding and restricting me from barely getting a breath of air. If we hadn't left, I don't even want to know what I would have become.

Child Care

We moved in with my wife's parents in Hawaii, and the change was so refreshing. My wife and I had a new season in life. She was resuming work shortly, the children would attend a new school, and I would have a fresh start. Within about two months, the school started up, and we were so excited. We thought that since it was a charter school, the children would be challenged. Unfortunately, this was almost the opposite of their previous school: students were getting into fights, the curriculum presented seemed about two grades behind, and everyone seemed like a number. The cost of living was high, and to put our children in a private school would have been around $2000 a month. The situation rode on the highway of becoming toxic, and we had to check out other options.

My wife had homeschooled our son, Timothy, for kindergarten with a Bible-based education, so I thought this might be a quick fix. But within a few minutes, it became evident that I wouldn't be able to drink and smoke around them, and they would be home with me all day. There had to be another way.

I called the old charter school up and even had my parents make an appearance. They worked with us, and miraculously a spot opened up. We flew back to my hometown, and the children made it to the first day of school just in time. This school year would mean some significant sacrifices. Our house was rented, my wife was committed to her new job for the school year, helping high needs children and her going back to graduate school full time. My children and I would spend the school year at my parents' house.

What a relief! I wouldn't have to give up my addictions, and my parents were loving enough to let us stay in their home. They even gave us two bedrooms and made it comfortable. Not that I needed a bed because I spent most of my time outside drinking and smoking. It was so painful to be sober, and I could hardly stand talking with anyone directly without a drink, an electronic device, and a cigarette.

The Almighty used my parents to wake me up from my addiction slumber. My father would persuade me to read, watch, or listen to positive and inspirational things. My mother always set a good example for the children and would take them to church. It was wonderful; they allowed us to share their home with them!

One family at the school was kind enough to invite my children to church with them on Wednesday nights. This reoccurrence used to bother me because it was another moment that the Almighty was trying to get my attention. I wasn't doing anything to teach my children the truths I had learned, so he allowed other people to step in. It was as if he was saying, "Karl, if you don't want to teach them, someone else will…and if you don't change, they will be even more lost than you are."

I felt even more backed into a corner. Something had to change. I couldn't go on living like this for it was a terrible example for my children, and horrible enough for my health. I knew it was time to go back and pick up where I left off six years ago.

TURN

But if a wicked man turns from all his sins which he has committed, keeps all My statutes, and does what is lawful and right, he shall surely live; he shall not die. None of the transgressions which he has committed shall be remembered against him; because of the righteousness which he has done, he shall live.

(Ezekiel 18:21-22)

In an attempt to change my course of life, I eliminated some major addictions. This process allowed me to, at least, have some peace. I spent a great deal of time in prayer and listening to many lessons on the internet. There are a lot of false teachers with convincing arguments. I imagined myself as Pontius Pilate, asking the Son of the Almighty, "What is truth?"

Because I trusted most of the Bible, I used the books of the laws, prophets, and writings to build upon, in a direction that supported this foundation. What helped me work through this was going to the source of people whose ancestors twrote these books. Which directions did they go nearly 2000 years ago, and where were they today? These descendants of Abraham, Isaac, and Jacob are the living proof of the Bible's very existence! Who better to observe and learn from? In my previous adventures, I had met World War II survivors of the Bataan Death March. How much more impressive it was to meet a survivor of the children of Jacob? Going to them for clarification helped me understand why they believed in the books of the New Covenant, and how they taught them was so convincing. One of the most healing verses was from the very books I had once doubted.

> *. . . We should no longer be children, tossed to and fro and carried about with every wind of doctrine, by the trickery of men, in the cunning craftiness of deceitful plotting, but, speaking the truth in love, may grow up in all things into Him who is the head—Christ...*
>
> (Ephesians 4:14-15)

Beginning My Journey with the Almighty

For nearly four months, I researched and concluded that the whole Bible was true and applicable in my life. This conclusion allowed me to use the rule of two or more witnesses in the Bible to back up what I was being taught. There are so many "rabbit trails" and "rabbit holes" that wasted my time and even changed my thinking, leading me onto a dead-end path. I still went down the lane to indulge, and every time I would pick myself up and turn around and try another way. It was a process of elimination, very similar to what I had done in my previous studies. Only this time, I used high-speed internet and advanced quickly through so many teachings, theologies, doctrines, and even debates. It was incredible how much information was available, and I could pick up where I left off years ago.

Again, here I reached the same crossroads as before. My lifestyle had experienced tremendous change. I knew that my vote in life was based on each action I did daily. I would now begin stepping out in faith.

Finally coming up for air: countless hours of research, some trial and error, and personal prayer schedules, all to prove the validity of the Bible. I was trying to see who was speaking the truth and possibly even doing things "right." What I concluded was only He, the Almighty Himself, is right. This allowed me to look directly to the Almighty in any circumstance on what He says is always true. There were some translation issues and even some passages of scriptures that caused questions to still arise. I diligently sought

Him daily in the Bible and took time to go back to the direct sources of the translations. Once I looked at the Hebrew or Greek texts, I saw the Bible interprets itself!

Now I was reading the Bible with "open eyes!" Researching what I had learned and comparing thought to thought, insight to insight, interpretation to interpretation, to see if it lines up with the words of the Almighty. I could understand that much of what I knew was taught to me, and it contradicted. I needed to stop listening to every 'teacher' and be a good disciple of the Word. Doing this would take much of the attention away from any person, and put the focus directly back to The Living Source Himself!

While researching and turning back to the Almighty, I let go of my addictions to video games and social media. Slowly I would delete one game after another and gave more time to the Almighty. Eventually, I even gave up my social media accounts. I thought about keeping them, but there were so many pulls from different directions I didn't want the distractions, and influences, anymore. It was sad not to see what my friends were doing. Still, with my addictive behavior, it was absolutely necessary if I wanted to develop a real relationship with our Creator.

WALK BY FAITH

But do you want to know, O foolish man, that faith without works is dead?

(James 2:20)

After rigorous attempts to attain the truth about the Almighty, the shadows gave way, and His shining bright light was being revealed. My understanding was forming from the habits of obedience to The Word.

As the Bible says, *"Faith without works is dead..."* and I was finally going to take action and do something, regardless of what others might think of me. Even if it was awkward, and I had a history of mistakes, I gave my best every day and slowly improved. At this point, I was already near rock bottom, but I believed I was stepping in the right direction. But how? How could I live out the Word? I lacked in so many areas. I needed all the help I could lay my hands on.

I remembered the Son of the Almighty said He would send a helper and that we could be one with Him just as He is one with His Father.

So I prayed and asked for this help. I received what I would best describe as a fire of motivation inside of me! Reading the Bible with fresh eyes and with increased belief made a significant impact. I would now read a scripture verse like, "Our body is a temple…" and was convicted by the Set-Apart Spirit to change my ways. In one night, I gave up cigarettes, beer, coffee, video games, meat, using profane words, and some other horrible things. Some of these things may not be considered wrong to do, but it was revealed to me that they were connected to the wrong things. For example, the coffee increased my desire to smoke cigarettes, and smoking increased my desire to drink beer. Drinking increased my desire to get drunk. If I were drunk, I would not be in the right mindset to grow and transform anew.

My Aptitude for Change

That same week, I decided to try and keep a Sabbath day. I didn't know what this would entail, but I had a powerful desire to do it. I spent most of the day resting, as that was what seemed most evident. I also enjoyed reading through the Bible. It seemed like at this time in my walk, I had a superpower and could read through whole books without stopping. I was so hungry for the truth and guidance on how to live correctly.

I spent more quality time with my children. Anything I learned was shared with them, and we would try and apply it to our lives. I woke up early and took my children to school. My mother used to drive them to school, but now I would take time to share with them what I was studying. I would even quiz them on it later as I dropped them off each day. We memorized The Ten Commandments, the order of the days of creation, and the Almighty's Set Apart Days. We all bought new Bibles and would share what we were learning with one another. I was very excited about this change!

My children shared with their friends at school. My son even took his Story Bible from home and would read it during his free time. Both the children became excited and shared with others about what we were, not only learning but doing! This new lifestyle became contagious, and my zeal was transferred right over to my children. Some of their classmates' parents were approaching me and shared that they noticed a big difference in them. The most significant difference I would say is that we couldn't keep quiet about the Almighty. To this day, we still talk about Him throughout the day; and think about Him all day, too!

With all the changes, my children and I could see ourselves in the stories of the Bible. We had escaped a spiritual Egypt and were out in the wilderness. We had received the Almighty's instructions and guidelines and were trying our best to learn and do them. Even though I had given up many addictive behaviors, there was still much work to do. The more I read, the more I changed. I believe it was as if the Almighty Himself had personally written me a letter. Not some cute little get well soon card, but a legitimate message on how to live and how to love Him and others in the Earth.

His words cut right through the barriers in my life. Shackles of addictions were broken almost instantly! I had tried for years to break these addictions and was like a dog who returned to his own vomit. But now, I saw the benefit of following the Almighty's instructions. The relationship with my children was alive in a whole new way. I was no longer trying to appease them with toys and electronics; but instead, spent time talking, laughing, and sharing meals. The Sabbath day was our big day to rest and focus on Him as a family. This time was my chance to teach my children as I learned, and to dwell together in unity.

Another significant change I made was that I read the Bible to my children every night. Not the adult Bible, but story Bibles where we could read a story together as a family and finish it each night. While doing this, I would stop and elaborate on things I had learned in my studies. The children asked so many questions, but I didn't mind. I just considered this was making up for the lost time and studying together. We got our 'Daily

Bread' and grew a little each day. Sometimes we would come across parts in the story Bible that didn't pan out or line up with what we believed. These incidents caused us to stop and look it up in the Bible, and often we found they were correct, and we would have to change our thinking. Other times when we looked things up, and they did not align, we realized someone's idea was added to the story; and that we would consider it but not hold it as accurate.

The Almighty equipped me by strengthening me with His powerful Word, the same with my children. We called my wife Jacqueline on the phone every day and would talk about the things we learned. This separation was a challenging time as she was swamped with work all day and going to school at night. We would talk during her commutes and shared as much as we could.

My parents were so thrilled their son was free from all these addictions. They had been very supportive and encouraging each time I tried to quit before the moment, but now it was an instant miracle right in their own home! I'm sure it was a prayer answered for them. They probably still thank the Almighty for today! We talked more and even shared during various Bible studies.

As the children and I progressed in our understanding, we wanted to recognize and keep the other appointed days of the Almighty. We learned about each day as they were approaching and took time off to celebrate. This process allowed us to see how relevant they are in understanding the Almighty and His Son. The first one after the weekly Sabbath was Passover and Unleavened Bread. My parents were kind enough to let me host a dinner at their house. We recognized the day of Passover with a few people present to celebrate: my parents, my sister, and my family. This event allowed me an excellent opportunity to learn and teach on a larger scale. We understood precisely why the Son of the Almighty died for our salvation and how *the leaven*, symbolic of sin, is necessary to be removed from our lives, to rightfully live. We didn't have any leaven in the house before that dinner and kept it out for seven days. We recognized all the other appointed days at their appointed times: the Feast of Weeks (Pentecost), the Day of Trumpets, the Day of Atonement, and the Feast of Tabernacles. So much was learned this year, and recognizing these special days helped us visualize how the Son of the Almighty is throughout the Bible. We were growing closer to the Almighty but also becoming closer as a family.

CLEANSE THE TEMPLE

Do you not know that to whom you present yourselves slaves to obey, you are that one's slaves whom you obey, whether of sin leading to death, or of obedience leading to righteousness?

(Romans 6:16)

Moving the Leaven

As our faith and commitment grew, so did the need to clean out more things in our lives. When we were preparing for The Feast of Unleavened Bread, we realized that it wasn't just the leaven in the house that was the issue. It included many thoughts, ideas, things, and rituals we used to do that were no longer comfortable. The Almighty said He is set apart, and we wanted to be set apart from who we were, too! This idea led us to eliminate anything that seemed contradictory to the Word of the Almighty.

My son was addicted to video games and would sometimes play an entire day during the weekend. My daughter was addicted to shopping and collecting toys. I could see this habit was an escape from reality, and they saw that it was as well. They wanted to be free, and we prayed about it, and gradually, they lessened their grip on their addictions, taking it a little at a time. First, we got rid of the things that were dishonoring to the Almighty. Then we moved on to the ones we thought might be dishonoring and let them go too. This method eased the process, and with my long-term holiday, I had availed the opportunity to remove the "leaven." Such a wonderful gift from the Almighty Himself. I could step up to become the father I desired to become.

Timothy's Leaven

My son, Timothy, was not overly excited about giving up so much of his video games. Some were not only pacifiers, but they were in the form of idol worship. I had to talk with him for a long time about the last few games as he saw them more as a way of keeping the door open to this addiction. I wanted him fully dedicated to the Almighty, so I had to be firm and gentle at the same time. We spent a lot of time in prayer and focusing our thoughts on the Almighty to ensure he didn't fall back. It was painful at first, but the Almighty stepped in and continued showing us where we needed change. Eventually, he completely healed my son!

I stepped up the ladder and moved from a dad that never was available, to one that was home every day, that I dared to encourage them to give up what they loved. These devices kept us enslaved from spending time together and learning how to live genuinely. The children wanted my time, and now they had it. We were busy cleaning up our lives and becoming a real family!

Quieting the Media

Another major area of the cleanup in our lives was what we watched and listened to. If we wanted to hear the Almighty's voice, we needed to minimize the noise of the influencing forces. The television and internet sources were sounding much different than before. I now recognized them as programming devices that could feed my family and me with information, both good and evil.

The news was a big distraction. It affected my thoughts, my time, and even my mood. Before, I was going to a human source to figure out what is going on in this world. Most of the information was very negative, full of gossip, and division. To this day, the people close to me know that unless there is a major catastrophe in the world or a new national leader appointed, don't bother telling me the news. I don't have time to hear everyone's opinions on today's situation. I want the

Almighty to show me what I need to do each day and speak to me, not someone telling me *this* or *that* situation is hopeless. The Almighty says that all things are possible. Mountains of fear and confusion can be moved out of my life! I found that seeking His Kingdom first and His Righteousness, there is complete peace within and understanding of all situations in our world.

Another significant change was eliminating physical programming that influenced us to want and desire things. My daughter used to watch shows based on shopping and unpacking toys. This lifestyle seemed acceptable and right, but now we could see the influence of always wanting more things. Toys and shopping fancies cluttered her room, her thoughts, and even her actions. She was obsessed with certain toys and characters in shows. Without being mindful of it, she also dressed and talked like some of them. As she cleaned out her room and cleared off the programming in her heart, her thoughts became more focused on the Almighty and family. Instead of wanting to use a toy oven to make a snack, she had the time and desire to help prepare meals for the whole family!

My wife and I cut out movies and shows with anything that was upsetting to the Almighty. If He was disgusted and upset by these things, we now were too. At first, this was sad because there were a lot of "good" movies and TV shows that were very interesting. Right in the middle of them, there would be an unnecessary scene that would cause us to turn it off. Sometimes it was a particular speech or action in the story that was inappropriate and wasn't being corrected. This tolerance could no longer be accepted as the Spirit in me was disgusted with these things.

Even our taste in music was different. Most of the time, we would drive in the car with no sounds. It seemed like every time I would put some music on, I would hear a word or a sound that no longer felt right. They indeed became distractions from thinking clearly. If I wanted to hear something, I would usually listen to a teaching or a message by another Believer. Often, I would listen to The Bible on CD and plant the Words of the Almighty in my mind and heart.

PLOW THE LAND

*H**umble yourselves in the sight of the Lord, and He will lift you up.*

(James 4:10)

I had become very obsessed with the Almighty and His instructions. Several months had passed now, and in this new lifestyle, we were continuing to grow closer to Him. We meticulously followed the process of understanding His Word, studying with open eyes, receiving hearts and minds. Although I realized something essential was missing in all my walk, which I did not recognize immediately – I lacked humility.

I needed to look to see if my heart and mind were fertile land to plant good seeds. I had received much of the Almighty's word and turned from my wicked ways. There were many "stones in the soil," and many "pebbles" that needed to be removed.

A Right Cause, a Wrong Approach

I noticed that as I shared with others, it was as if the Almighty Himself showered me with divine understanding. People who seemed sincere with a burning passion for knowing the Almighty were doing things that seemed contradictory to the Bible. I thought they were "lost," and maybe they were, but my actions showed no desire to be compassionate to reach to them where they were lacking. Instead, I told them how they were "wrong" in their thinking. This instructing wasn't something I enjoyed doing. Still, I was so zealous for the Almighty's righteousness I would correct loved ones, with firm answers.

Some scriptures would come into my thoughts and penetrated into my heart to change my ways. I would hear, "Grievous words stir up anger…," or "The tongue is a member that can defile the whole body." It was time to take action and learn how to love my neighbor as myself.

I learned how to love people other than my own flesh and blood for the first time. Initially, the process of humility was happening toward my children and me. Still, towards others, I was a little bit hardened. I remembered that the Almighty wouldn't even accept our offerings if we aren't right with our brothers first.

There's a parable about a man who was forgiven a substantial debt by his master and then wouldn't do the same to his fellow servant; this was considered wicked. The Almighty was giving me grace, but I failed to provide the same to others. These scriptures were cutting deep into my heart and mind. My fleshly claws would have to let go of this evil if I wanted to be forgiven and grow into maturity.

So, the issues to work on were obvious now; false pride and forgiveness. I genuinely believe that the Almighty's grace was given to me up to this point, and now He was exposing things for me to work on one step at a time. When I started, I needed that grace to get me to where I could be healed, that I could love myself, and also love Him enough to realize these things. But this false image I had created of myself over the decades needed to die completely. Much of my pride was caused by the hurt I felt deep within: certain people who did me wrong, situations that ended badly, or my health turning and feeling restricted. These issues were coming up into thoughts, and some I didn't even know how to let go. I would often contemplate, "I forgave this person, but why do I revisit those memories?" Or, "the Almighty has blessed me with time and desire to know Him, why am I so concerned about my health?"

A big part of my growth in these areas was getting back into my own home. Even with my health issues, I realized that living under the same roof with my parents made it difficult to become who the Almighty was transforming me to be. I needed some space to be free, teach my children, and create new habits that complimented what the Creator was leading us to do.

A Direction from the Almighty

At first, I wanted to move back into our home in Colorado, but it was still rented out. Besides, that infamous porch would be howling at me at night and calling out to me in the day. Thousands of hours of bad habits performed daily in the past, and the idea was feeling heavy and dangerous. I prayed to the Almighty and asked for His guidance on where to go. The other place I was considering was Hawaii. Jacqueline was already there doing meaningful work and going to graduate school. Her parents had enough room as well, and we were welcomed. Unfortunately, the same memories of my bad habits were practiced there too. I needed a fresh start with as little distractions as possible.

Every time I looked for a place to move, there was a strong urge towards Oklahoma. This state was somewhere I had spent very little time and knew no one. Thoughts of the mile-wide tornado flattening the houses in 1999 crossed my mind. I didn't like that there were no mountain ranges or oceans to view either. But my wife and I would be buying a place that felt like the middle of nowhere. Despite the worldly warnings, I was led by the Spirit to sojourn there until further guidance from the Almighty. And just like Abraham, we did!

The closing on this property was the longest I had ever experienced. For some reason, the lender decided to verify Jacqueline's income that morning. They were in Missouri, and she was in Hawaii, so her workplace wasn't even open for several hours into the early morning closing. Around the fifth or sixth hour, I remember the sellers' agent losing patience and composure. I could understand the frustration as we were experiencing it too. We even had a flight to catch. What really surprised me was how my six-year-old daughter and nine-year-old son could sit in there and not complain once. The old Chloe and Timothy wouldn't have lasted five minutes without a doll or video game, but they now knew there was more to life than themselves. I wish the adults that day could have learned that lesson from my children. But the evidence of the Almighty in our lives was more evident now than ever!

Following the Good Shepherd

After we moved into our new home, I understood that one of the people who killed the Son of the

Almighty was myself. I used to say it was the people of old who were blind that caused His death. But at this moment, I realized that He freely gave His life so we, the rebellious ones, might have eternal life. His very name itself means "salvation." I also took some time to study the sacrificial system and how He became our High Priest in Heaven, sitting at the right hand of His Father. I could now see more clearly the cost of my actions. I wanted to be worthy of hearing, "Well done, good and faithful servant." Still, instead, I was guilty of not forgiving others and not being responsible for my actions. I did not differ from Adam in the Garden of Eden, who blamed his wife. My spiritual growth was at a point in the road where I needed a boulder removed. Without this change, I would be living as a hypocrite and a blind guide to my family.

Once I listened to a brother speak about certain kinds of grace at work in people's lives, he had people placed under two major umbrellas. Those who shielded in the world of "hyper-grace" merely accepted the Son of the Almighty as their savior. Nothing changed in their lives, then the "hyper-law," where everyone follows the law to the letter, and there is no grace.

By examining my life with these words, I was one of the latter, and the very laws that gave me an understanding of the Almighty Himself, also caused me to live without love. As a pendulum swings, so did I.

From the childhood of asking forgiveness and salvation, to now doing works to justify my salvation. I noticed I lacked the most crucial ingredient in my faith walk, as I did not have a good mentor! Once the sermon ended, I realized this excellent teacher was the Son of the Almighty Himself. It was the Anointed One Who spoke to me Himself through the man. It felt as if a second veil had been removed from my eyes! I could see how He loved His Father and His neighbor flawlessly while He stayed on earth. By applying the entire Word of the Almighty, I could remove these stones grounded in my heart.

The situation reminded me of how the Son of the Almighty corrected men who wanted to stone a woman for adultery, without the other guilty party. They wanted partial justice without mercy, yet how many times in history has the Almighty given us His mercy? The other guilty party was not present for the stoning. Just a day before the Son of the Almighty had told them He was the living water, yet they refused to drink because of their lack of belief in Him. I now believed in Him at a whole new level. He became my master and shepherd, and I became His bondservant.

Never relenting, I wanted this mercy so much and put myself in other people's shoes. I tried to stop looking at how much better I was doing but instead focused on how far I was from the Son of the Almighty.

He's the one I was supposed to be following, of course! Leaning not on my own understanding and realizing there is more to the stories throughout life. He alone gives perfect judgment because He has all the information. He is The Word, He is The Door, He is The Living Water, and everything I'll ever need. I was deeply convinced that the Almighty would move that giant boulder in the road, and I would be on a better, straighter path. This mustard seed faith would begin to move mountains!

PLANT THE SEEDS

But he who received seed on the good ground is he who hears the word and understands it, who indeed bears fruit and produces: some a hundredfold, some sixty, some thirty.

(Matthew 13:23)

It became evident that if anyone were going to see the greatness happening on the inside, I would have to plant seeds that produce good fruits. I listened to the voice of the Almighty's word, and it was impossible to produce good and bad fruit at the same time. Sometimes, negative thoughts would come into my mind, and I had to consciously change them to upright ones. Any time I was looking at the Almighty's commandments, I studied to see how His Son handled them.

Spiritual Strength for Mental Weakness

Such as I said, like the way I checked out my diet, I was becoming more cautious about what I allowed into my life. I was intentional about what I watched, read, listened to, and even who I gave my time. I realized that I wasn't there to change lives, but only the Almighty was. I was to satisfy my idleness while I removed the "leaven" from my own life first, and roll back from ingesting it while in the wilderness. I made analogies of my situation as that of the Biblical scenes of Abraham, leaving his family in Haran, or the children of Israel learning in the wilderness. I was getting to know the Almighty on a personal level. Every time I would go through one of these changes, I had to re-read the Living Word again. This process allowed a new understanding to be planted in my mind and heart. I was connecting the many dots throughout the entire Bible. I watered them with prayer and continuously asked for the Set-Apart Spirit, to be with me. This way, I was being led by the Spirit and planting good seeds on humble soil.

Around that time, we had an incident that challenged my faith and exposed the growth happening on the inside. I had stepped out the front door for a minute, and when I returned, sounds of chaos filled the house. My daughter was screaming with tears flowing. The neighbor's dalmatian was in our laundry room! The dog was barking franticly, and our tiny kitten was between the washer and dryer with hair and whiskers fully extended. My son had just moved the washer and dryer apart a few weeks prior because he felt led to. This made no sense at all until this moment. Instant rage filled my thoughts, but almost simultaneously, a new source from within reminded me to love my neighbor.

I firmly grabbed the dog and took him back to the neighbor's house. They had the most technologically savvy doorbell I had ever seen! This device called their cell phone and also had a camera so they could see my sweaty face and their misbehaved dog. Fortunately, they unlocked the door remotely, and I put the dog in their house. They were at a party and wouldn't be home for hours. Once I exited the house, they were still talking and asked if I would put the dog in the kennel in the office. I couldn't believe it! The old me tried to come up and tell them, "No way, your dog, your problem!" But fortunately, the Set-Apart Spirit stepped in and followed their request. I even made sure the door remotely locked before going home.

After going home, I noticed my daughter had scratches all over her hands and arms and was bleeding. While cleaning up her wounds, I learned the dog had broken in through the fence and stood up on the back door to open the lever. If this were a house fire, I would have been all for it; but this was a new one. I remembered that I had talked to the neighbor a few weeks before the dog was chewing the boards, that he needed to replace pickets on the fence. I had even offered to pay half. He let me know he'd take care of it, but nothing happened. I held my daughter for quite a few hours longer and thanked the Almighty for teaching me His ways.

This was my time to shine as a Believer and show love to my neighbor. I was setting a good example for my children to follow. The seeds planted in me were now taking root and holding on during trying times. I could now have peace and joy in challenging circumstances.

Wow! I was now in a whole different mindset and ready to take my family to the next level—homeschooling! My children were a little hesitant at first because they were in a respectable school and doing very well. They also had their friends and, most importantly, an opportunity to witness to others. This decision was a hard one because the children were not convinced of the idea, and I was not feeling physically, nor academically qualified. Could this same guy that was a former drunk and brain-damaged individual truly step out and step up to this occasion? Everything in my fleshly self said no, but every part of my spirit said, "Yes!" It was another test I would have to deal with and a real chance to plant beautiful seeds in my children's lives.

So my little seedlings and I were now on a mission to turn not only our free time into honoring the Almighty but academics as well. The Almighty granted me wisdom, and I saw a way through the pending wilderness. Admittedly, I attended a Bible-based school for first and second grade, so I dutifully researched their programs. It turned out they offered a homeschool curriculum, much like what I had used, but with a few updates. This news was very encouraging because the curriculum would allow the children to work independently, and I would be more of a supervisor and test proctor. This way, when I had a "bad" day physically, my children would still be able to complete their assignments, while I could rest and recover. What a blessing this was turning out to be. They even offered a short course for teachers where I could learn how to set up the classroom and respond to student's questions. I learned how to help the children solve their own problems, and so many other great ideas on how to be effective. We had the whole summer to get moved into our new home, set the classroom up, and order all the books.

At first, the children were excited because they could work at their own pace and finish school rather quickly. But after a few weeks, I noticed they needed physical and everyday skills to be taught. Things like how to cook, clean properly, make a budget, write a letter, set goals, and make plans; another hidden blessing! Now I could teach them skills that would make them successful and independent. The children also attended gymnastics classes for exercise and confidence.

Now the homeschool was turning into a tight-knit team! We started our school after breakfast and would recite scriptures along with a short lecture. I realized this was a huge opportunity; my children at home with me with their undivided attention. So, I would talk to them about life-applicable topics just before they did their studies, but in the classroom setting. We had resources like our Bibles, desks, and a whiteboard to enhance the lecture. We put the topic into an applicable real-life scenario. We also had time to eat all our meals together and help each other throughout the day. If I wasn't well, they could help me and still keep up with all their studies. We became servants to each other and were beginning to die to our selfishness a little more each day.

Some people seemed concerned the children would not have any social skills. This idea made me laugh to myself because what kind of socialization do you think a child needs more of; how to talk and behave like other children or their parents? Who do you want your child to be influenced by, another peer or their mentor? My response out loud to the other person was, "Do you think I'm unsocial?" It was comical but very concerning. I also would share how King Solomon's son should have listened to the elders instead of his peers.

Much of my childhood issues were due to peer pressure. Even in Bible-based schools, there were many different influences from unique families. Also, in churches, I remember meeting many people who had some interesting, worldly ideas. Therefore, I was convinced if I wanted to ensure I diligently taught my children the Almighty's ways. The seed planting was to be done at home throughout the day and night. Regardless of what other people thought, I had to do what the Almighty was convicting me to do. I would continue pressing on in the race. I didn't want to waste this opportunity that the Almighty had given me—my time. Seeds need time to grow, and the right environmental conditions.

WASHED IN THE WORD DAILY

Be diligent to present yourself approved to God, a worker who does not need to be ashamed, rightly dividing the word of truth.

(2 Timothy 2:15)

A dear friend of ours agreed to watch over our two dogs, Oliver and Bella, until we were settled in another house. For a year and a half, she took care of them and often had us over for dinner; her food and laughs were a pure delight. She took exceptional care of our dogs, and somehow they always knew we were coming over.

One time while visiting, I noticed next to her evening chair was her heavily used Bible. Never had I heard her talk about the Almighty, but I wasn't surprised to see this. Her actions spoke loud of her love for others, and when I brought up the Almighty, she invited me to a Bible study. From that point on, she was very open about Him, and I could see He was her source of life.

The way she loved was beyond evident that she was a true bondservant of the Anointed One.

With this said, you could imagine how hard it was for me to inform her we were ready to take the dogs back. I knew both her and the dogs had become very close, but I needed to take accountability.

Timothy and Chloe both agreed they wanted to be more helpful and take on more responsibility. So we met halfway and made a speedy trip. As sad as it was to take the dogs away from her, you should have seen the lit-up faces of my children. No more leaving all the dog messes for mom, we were now ready to do our duty. Same with the brushing and feeding. We were so grateful for what our friend had done. She cared for the dogs and showed us what a real Believer in the Almighty acts like.

A significant change took place in my life and family, day after day. We had lots of time to work together while we learned how to dwell together in unity. After all, we did not only enjoy the current benefits of our new life in the Anointed One, we also harnessed the eternal benefits too.

Most days became a routine, and there were times I found my patience was near the end. Our complacency for something we loved was turning to boredom. We absorbed the new lifestyle we just received, but needed an occasional reminder of the wonderful gift of freedom from addictions. I learned to fall forward each time I fell off the highway of righteousness. I quickly repented and bounced right up every time. I needed to hear what the Almighty had to say daily. Perhaps, it was a sermon, reading of the Bible or prayer, I was up for much guidance and correction to mold me into an outstanding example to my family.

Bible Study with a Congregation

I spent much of my free time with my children, learning our brand-new lifestyle. We would watch a lot of studies online from many different congregations, and we never got tired. We would even visit any of the physical churches along with some other Worshipers, who we also learned from. One group had invited me to a Bible study on Wednesday nights while the children were taught in another room. I was all for this at first, because I wanted us to get out to encourage, and be inspired by other Believers. This desire only lasted about three weeks, and I couldn't do it anymore. I wanted to, but in my spirit, it seemed wrong and inconvenient. What bothered me was that the Bible study group never opened the Bible! We had to pay $10 for a book by some author I didn't know and watch his videos and answer questions in a workbook. I had done similar studies like this before, but this end-times study was not lining up with the Word of the Almighty. I frowned inside, and every part of me wanted to immediately revolt at the indiscipline. In the last class I attended, when we went around the room to share, I opened my Bible and read:

Not everyone who says to Me, "Lord, Lord," shall enter the kingdom of heaven, but he who does the will of My Father in heaven. Many will say to Me in that day, "Lord, Lord, have we not prophesied in Your name, cast out demons in Your name, and done many wonders in Your name?" And then I will declare to them, "I never knew you; depart from Me, you who practice lawlessness!"

(Matthew 7:21-23)

I said I consider this preparation for "end times." I wanted to work out my salvation with fear and trembling. I left it at that but wanted to share more. Never would I want to cause division, nor confusion. I would only share His words and let Him do His work.

The Almighty revealed that His Word is more important than my opinions. His Word always interprets itself. He gave me the knowledge that time of playing "book club" and having drinks and snacks would not bring me closer to Him. If I wanted to witness to others, I needed to get to know Him personally.

Family Bible Study

I bought a new Bible to use, specifically for studying. A Bible I could highlight and write in all my notes and thoughts. It had no references in it, nor any commentary. This Bible would build up my research ability. At that time, I had some minor surgery done and wouldn't be walking much for a while. This was an excellent time to dig into the Word. It was as if the Almighty Himself was telling me to stay home and study. I went line by line and would ask myself, "What does this mean and how can I apply this to my life today?" I was getting more out of this than the hundreds of sermons and teachings I had listened to before. Many of those teachings were necessary, but most of what they were sharing was coming right from the source!

This process took me a little over a year. Still, the Almighty blessed me with incredible wisdom and understanding I never dreamed existed. Sometimes I would study for four hours a day, but most of the time, I found it better to learn to a standard, not to a set time. My son read through his Bible like this, too, and we had incredible discussions on thousands of topics. His mind was good at remembering specific details, and our nightly Bible studies were at a whole new level of understanding.

During this time, my mother came to visit us for a few weeks. We had several Bible studies together and many discussions. She has always read her Bible, and the wisdom and understanding she brought to the group were much appreciated. What she shared with me has stuck with me to this day. She said that doing family Bible studies was an answer to her prayer from several decades before. This experience was something she wanted more with her children, but life got busy. We were having a historical moment of overcoming a generational challenge I didn't even know existed. My mother and father did their very best to raise me, and they trained me in many right ways. Now, we were becoming a bigger blessing for future generations.

My father used to bless me and say, "You will become more successful and do more than me, Karl…" His words caused me to believe like I was part of something important. I'll have greater wisdom to do much bigger things, and an overwhelming joy welled in my spirit. We were teaching our children diligently to train their future generations. I may have left the faith for several years, but now my obedience to the Almighty was leaving a mark of success for them. Persistent prayers from genuine parents were causing timeless blessings to pour over us. We were never blessed so much!

PRODUCING GOOD FRUIT

*B*ut *the fruit of the Spirit is love, joy, peace, longsuffering, kindness, goodness, faithfulness, gentleness, self-control. Against such there is no law. And those who are Christ's have crucified the flesh with its passions and desires. If we live in the Spirit, let us also walk in the Spirit.*

(Galatians 5:22-25)

At the time of my mother's visit, the Almighty also blessed us with another child. This news was a considerable shock because we thought we were done having children. Our youngest child then, Chloe, was seven years old, and welcoming a new baby was a drastic change. We recently bought a new house a few months before, and now my wife would have to stop working for a while. Furthermore, eight years earlier, we lost our second son, William, at birth. After that tragic moment in time, the doctors said Jacqueline had a high-risk pregnancy and, thus, was on bed rest. We were grateful for the Almighty's gift of life. We took the necessary precautions to ensure Jacqueline and the baby were safe. This time also allowed the children and me to share with her how much we had matured.

We became Jacqueline's servants, and it was a fantastic way to show her our new lifestyle of obedience. We helped look after the baby and after her. Looking back, I see that even when we did that, we grew so fast that the Almighty didn't want us to leave any family member behind. He wanted us to not only teach The Word of the Almighty to Jacqueline but to act it out in our works toward each other. I'm sure this was quite a shock for her after a whole year of working, going to graduate school, and visiting us only on the set-apart days. Now, she would live with us full time again. Also, the children and I were no longer the needy people asking her to do everything. There was no time for that; I had become a servant and a leader. The children were no longer addicted to the things of their past; they were obedient examples of our faith and belief in the Almighty. He was alive in us, and He had built us up for this very moment!

Timothy and Chloe were learning to cook meals on a higher level now. Before they would take a box of mac n' cheese and use the stovetop. Now, they were using cookbooks and following directions. To get to this level was a process that took several months of teaching and supervising. My patience and endurance to love were tested, and we all overcame together. The children enjoyed the time and attention as well. This education was preparing them for their future generations.

When no one was up for the challenge of cooking, we would go out to eat. This was something I loved doing for many years, as it was my way of taking a turn cooking. Jacqueline would often joke and say, "I love it when you cook, Karl!" We would all laugh and enjoy lots of various cuisines. Our income was limited now, so this was something we could only do once or twice a month. Before, we would go out a few times a week, but now we needed to simplify our lives.

One of the activities we would do as a family was going for short visits to the Oklahoma City Zoo and Botanical Gardens. The zoo had a lot to offer. Probably the most unusual scene for all of us was there was a citrus tree on their grounds. If we were still in Key West with our motorhome, no big deal, but here in the plains of middle America was a very odd sight. We talked with one of the employees, and they shared that the tree had the right nutrients, and that's why it was loaded with fruit. I wanted to be like that tree and surprise others with evident fruit, not from this world.

We wanted to be representatives of the Almighty through our acts and our words. We would let Jacqueline rest, bring her all her meals, and have our nightly Bible studies in the room where she was lying. We even bought her a large couch for the living room, so she could relax on something other than a bed, and be near us throughout the day. It was so pleasant to have her home full time again! We loved giving her what the Almighty had given us, His peace and mercy. It was a new chapter in our life. There were so many things that only the children's mother could give them, so now the team in this house was a complete family in this home!

One of our newest challenges was we had grown so fast, spiritually, that Jacqueline was at a different level than us. It was as if we were talking in a different language and probably even a little wordy to her. Often, she would fall asleep during the Bible studies and have nothing to share. I felt sad and responsible for her disinterest. I wanted to see her grow and experience the peace and understanding we were receiving. I also wanted her to step into the role of a Proverbs 31 wife, that would be an excellent example for our children.

I was now experiencing what 'dying to myself daily' was like—spending time diligently teaching my children to love the Almighty and love others. I made them work together so they would understand they were a part of something bigger than themselves. Most of our free time was now spent helping around the house and helping Jacqueline get comfortable. Many days I had nothing to give and felt like giving up. After all, I still had many health challenges and had every reason to use them as an excuse. But I knew that the Almighty could make up where I had nothing to give. He was with me!

Often, my back would hurt and go out. I would pray, "Heavenly Father, please help me to move so I can serve, You don't even have to take away the pain, just please help me move so I can be an example to my family. Let Your name be glorified, not mine." And you know what? He helped me! He would help me move, and sometimes even take away the pain.

There was a pattern becoming evident to me now. Every time the Almighty helped me overcome a challenge, another one would be revealed. I desired to continue being pressed like an olive, to produce oil to burn and let His light shine through me. This fruit was the kind I wanted to give to my wife, my children, and, most of all, to the Almighty Himself.

EMBRACING THE BODY OF BELIEVERS

*...**B**ehold, how good and how pleasant it is For brethren to dwell together in unity!*

(Psalm 133:1)

After several weeks of Jacqueline being reunited with us, we attended a congregation I was following online. I thought this might be an opportunity for Jacqueline to grow more spiritually by being around other Believers. We went for a few weeks, but it didn't last. The services were late in the evenings, and in my spirit, I didn't feel right about being there. The children were showing a lack of discipline, and it seemed like I was too.

A Truth About Giving

Subsequently, I found another congregation I was following online in which their sermons were

97

similar to the way we believed. I decided we should visit them too. The children and I had visited them a few times before and were blessed but didn't feel led to be there. It was as if the Almighty wanted us to Himself, to teach us through His Spirit and His Words. I truly believed He wanted all the glory for helping us to overcome. It may have looked funny that I returned to the congregation to help encourage my wife to join us in our way of living fully. I thought that seeing other Believers doing these things would help, and it did!

We attended the new member's class and learned more about giving. Being a whole Bible-believing congregation, I shouldn't have been surprised, but this was an area I needed revelation. Before this point, I didn't give my money to the Almighty unless it was to help someone in need. I thought that money was an offering and optional. I also had a bad experience growing up in the church and seeing our pastor go to prison. He had stolen a considerable amount of the offerings. This left me questioning the integrity of spiritual leadership and the need to give. The Spirit of the Almighty worked in me. He revealed the importance of acknowledgment that everything comes from Him, even my money.

So, then, my wife wasn't working; we were less than a year into buying a new home, and now we are going to start to give our money? Financially, this was becoming very uncomfortable. Although, I was entirely convinced this was the right thing to do and was determined to make it work. For the first two months, I kept seeing our money go into the negatives. I prayed to the Almighty for peace and wisdom in this area. I also researched the topic further in the Bible.

Going through the different offerings in the Bible, I thought, "Maybe I'll find a loophole and won't need to do this anymore because I'm already short on money." Instead, what I found was, I should be giving about two and a third times more than what I was currently giving! This revelation was becoming a colossal test of faith. In my fleshly mind, I accepted defeat. I considered selling the house and even asked my wife, who was very pregnant at the time when she wanted to go back to work. I forgot about how the Son of the Almighty multiplied the bread and fish. It was as though I had just crossed the Red Sea and forgotten who was with me, the Almighty!

To this day, I cannot fully explain this, but when we were faithful to give the Almighty our first fruits, we began to be so blessed financially. Typical maintenance issues were becoming almost non-existent, food and fuel costs were going down, and we even received some checks in the mail. Apparently, we overpaid for the house and some other bills. Friends and family members would offer us food and money for no reason at all. I remember one time a person in the congregation gave me some money. I said, "Oh, no thanks, we are fine," but they refused to back down because they said the Almighty led them to do this. At that point, I couldn't say no to the Almighty, so I said, "Thank you." Then they looked at me sternly and said, "No, thank the Almighty!" Indeed, that is what I did. I thanked the Almighty for all His favor and blessing on my family's life financially. It was as if the Creator Himself was saying, "Karl, you keep your mouth shut, be blessed, keep faithful to my commands, and live!"

The sermons at the congregation always touched me as they were often about things I had recently overcome or were currently working on. One time I took a minute to thank the lead elder for such excellent teaching as I really felt encouraged. He quickly corrected me lovingly and said that it was the work of the Spirit that was talking directly to me. What a blessing!

Another wonderful blessing we received during that time was the birth of our youngest son, Yonathan; he was such a gift from the Almighty. He was so healthy, even healthier than our other three children at birth. I believe this was because we were living better and making choices that were more honoring to the Almighty.

While we were attending the congregation, I was continuing with my own online studies. One of the online gatherings had offered to start up a men's group where we could video chat with one another and have virtual Bible studies. I met so many Believers of various backgrounds and understandings. Some theological ideas were really strange to us, but with the strange also came anointed and seasoned Worshipers who were led by the Spirit.

One of the online applications we used was a program that allowed us to record a video message and then share it with the group. Some people would share a couple of times a week to give insight to what the Almighty was doing in their lives. It was exhilarating to be with such a devout group of men that wanted to talk about Him all day. I would often share verses that really touched me that day and sometimes participate in Bible studies.

After our son Yonathan was born, I became pretty close with one of the brothers. He knew how to motivate me and bring out the best in my personality. At first, I was communicating with him a few times a day, but within a few months, we were sometimes interacting for a few hours a day. In my spirit, I knew I had to throttle back with the time, but I kept finding myself giving more time to him than to the Almighty Himself.

It was an awkward situation. Because we were honoring the Almighty in our speech, but I knew I wasn't as devoted to reading my Bible and spending time with my family. My phone was now carried around the house like a bottle of life-giving water. Every notification became important. This was becoming a habit I needed to get control of quickly.

Another habit at that time was drinking coffee. When I first received the Set-Apart Spirit, I gave up coffee to help with the cravings of the other practices, but after a year, it seemed safe to drink again. I started having a cup in the mornings, and within a few months, I was drinking two pots every day! Now, I understood why I gave it up before and had to give it up again. My online brother was the primary motivator in this push, and I was grateful for his support.

About that time, the online group started doing Bible trivia on Sunday nights. This was super exciting! Our whole family played every week, and we called ourselves "Team Homeschool." We often placed on the leaderboard out of hundreds of seasoned Bible scholars, so we were feeling pretty animated. My son Timothy was like a cheetah out of the brush on its prey when answering these questions.

After several weeks of doing this, I noticed it not only messed with our sleep but our hearts. We were becoming prideful, and often when we didn't win, my son would become emotional. We decided it would be best to take a break from the competition and spend more time sleeping during those late hours.

So now I had the coffee habit nipped, and my late-night Bible parties under control, but I needed to deal with this online fellowship habit. My brother was very dear to me, as were all the other brothers, but he and I had grown so close it was difficult to tell him I needed to step back. When I did, he respected me, but I kept finding myself carrying the phone around and constantly checking it. I finally told all the brothers my situation and that I was going to disconnect from the group but was happy to chat on the phone occasionally.

My brother and I continued to stay in touch and even did Bible studies sometimes. After a few months, our communication dropped. He was now busy with new family health challenges, and I was often waiting for a call that never happened. Looking back, I can see he had some big priorities, but at the time, I became impatient with him. At one point, I even let him know I was disappointed. Unfortunately, it didn't go so well, but what I realize now is the Almighty was pulling me from him. Not for his sake, but for mine. The Almighty wanted me busy growing and spending more time with Him and my family.

A Compelling Dream

While we attended the congregation, we made some phenomenal friends. After three months of visiting there, I had a compelling dream. In the dream, I was at the place where we were meeting with the congregation. During the service, my daughter was being taken away, led astray, and nowhere to be found. The dream was so real that when I woke up, I had to go check to see if Chloe was in her bed. I asked the Almighty for guidance and understanding of the dream. Still, I never had a full interpretation, so no action was taken.

A few months after I had the dream, we were back in Colorado, visiting my family. My parents had a time-share in Breckenridge, so we spent a week relaxing in the fresh mountain air. At the condominium, there was an incident that triggered the alarm systems. Lights were flashing, and security guards were guiding people out by the masses. This unfortunate event caused such a panic in my wife, it was hard for her to be comforted. We had already experienced so much stress with the separation during combat deployments and work situations that Jacqueline could hardly take any more. Immediately the dream of my daughter came back to my memory. I realized that if something had happened at the place of meeting, it would be challenging to react: my wife was in the nursery, my daughter was in a children's class, and my son and I were in the sanctuary. There was so much separation in the large building, and it was feeling unsafe. This uncertainty is why we stopped attending.

When we stepped back from gathering with the congregation. I felt led to contact the congregation leader. I had so much respect for him and the people there and didn't feel right to just disappear saying nothing. I had new friends there that I wanted to talk to, but this dream was so intense I didn't want to share a spirit of fear with others, so I just let them know we were stepping away for now.

Before we finished our visit to Colorado, I had one morning I'll never forget! Our dog, Bella, pretended to be friendly with one of my dad's friends at the door and quickly made a mad dash for the streets. Unlike the home I grew up in, my parents now lived in town and could easily walk to businesses. I dropped everything I was doing at the moment and made my way out the door to find her. Between my dad's yells and seeing Bella's ears flying back in excitement, I took off at an exhilarating speed walk pace! She was gone!

A bustling street ahead and the screeching of car tires caught my attention. Bella wasn't like the dogs I had grown up with; she was a runner! About that time, a man approached with his dog, and I asked if he had seen

Bella. She mentioned she had seen the dog turn down the street (yes, he was a she). She helped me find Bella and was very friendly. After we located the little dog, I thanked her and went on my way, now holding Bella. I felt bad for judging the lady, but I was perplexed about her gender. I made a bad judgment call because I was thinking I was more righteous than her in my mind, but she proved me wrong by her good Samaritan actions. I hoped she had not noticed I was distressed. The Almighty was using her to teach me to look deep inside like the good Samaritan, not like the other two Believers. They walked right past the hurting man. To make matters more interesting, I realized that I was still in my house slippers and pajamas! These were not ordinary flannel patterns, either. Before Yonathan was born, my mother was so excited she made pajamas for my whole family. So here I stood in my baby blue two-piece homely attire. Now that you know more of the story, who do you think showed more love for their neighbor? Who do you think looked more out of place? What a humbling lesson on judging others!

For the next nine months, we would go back to studying and worshiping the Almighty from home. All that to say, I was grateful for the growth that happened over the last five months with such a loving congregation. We truly experienced the importance of sharing and receiving the fruits that the Almighty had helped us to produce.

TESTING MY FAITH

My brethren, count it all joy when you fall into various trials, knowing that the testing of your faith produces patience. But let patience have its perfect work, that you may be perfect and complete, lacking nothing.

(James 1:2-4)

Leaving the congregation felt like I had just gone through a loss of a loved one. We had found a place we could dwell together in unity. I continued listening to all the sermons from the congregation and giving our family's offerings online. I also prayed for the congregation every night, sometimes with tears. We were all growing together and learning how to be part of a community. I knew that I had my commitments to the Almighty and my family, and I would have to step it up.

At first, I was looking for another congregation that was smaller and more intimate. I thought that if we could all be in the same room; we wouldn't have a problem anymore; we would feel safe. In my mind, this made sense, but in my spirit, I thought about great

Believers in the Bible, who were brave and wouldn't let the fears of the world interfere with their worship of the Almighty. To me, worshiping the Almighty wasn't going to a place or being with a specific group of people. It was about a relationship with Him, and mine had been active for a year and a half now. I recalled that the reason we went visiting the congregation in the first place was to encourage my wife and even my daughter. I wanted them to be excited about the Sabbath, and worshiping the Almighty. In my heart, I knew that later in life, we should try to be with a congregation and continue seeking His Kingdom first. Still, the gathering itself starts with the family, not a building.

Jacqueline's parents invited us to visit with them for a few weeks in Hawaii, and we gladly accepted. It was so exciting to see her parents and the tropical environment again. Much of our time was spent eating grandma's delicious food and going to the beach.

One beach we really liked had extra soft sand and mild waves. The children were able to run out quite away without too much concern. During certain times of the day, tiny jellyfish would end up on the shore, and Chloe got stung. The incident terrified my daughter so badly that she didn't want to go near the beach anymore. She just stood on the hill above watching us, and every time I asked her to join us, she quickly declined.

After lots of encouragement and motivation, I convinced her to come back and keep enjoying the beach. She clung to me in fear for the first thirty minutes but finally realized she needed to live on and have faith she was safe, not a life of fear. This lesson on fear was not only for her but for me as well.

Responding to the Call

When we returned back to Oklahoma, we were refreshed and ready to continue working as a family. Our meals became very simple. Oatmeal every morning, peanut butter and jelly sandwiches for lunch, and dinner was usually a lovely meal cooked together, which often varied. Our goal was to make the dinner last for two days to save money and time. We no longer went out to eat once, or twice, a month. Instead, that money was used to help those less fortunate. When opportunities arose to help those in need, we always had money built up to assist. For example, a local organization sent out a request for diapers for orphans. We used that fund to purchase several boxes of diapers in various sizes and deliver to them. None of this would have been possible if we hadn't searched out in the Bible about offerings. When Jacqueline and the children gave them to the organization, the lady in the front was so excited! We had responded in record time! It wasn't our time, though, but instead being led by His Spirit, in His time! She asked which organization we were, and Jacqueline told her we were not representing any group. The lady's face dropped. She was amazed that a single family would be willing to do so much, and she got a camera to take a photo. Jacqueline kindly explained that it was unnecessary, but the lady insisted and talked Tim and Chloe into getting their picture.

On the ride home, Jacqueline told me about what had happened. I then realized the impact of being led by the Spirit. Those children wouldn't have to wait or go without. The Almighty led Jacqueline to that public announcement, and our obedience led us to live more simply so we could give. A few weeks later, I was listening to a local congregation online. They were making an announcement for diapers and was so glad to know we had responded to the Almighty when it was needed.

There were many other ways He directed us to do things with, and without, using money. One time He told me to take $20 and go early to my doctor's appointment and give it to a person in need. Excited to have a mission, I left about thirty minutes early and drove to the nearest Walmart parking lot. I had given money to the homeless before and assumed this is what He meant.

When I arrived at the parking lot, there was not a single homeless person in sight. I searched for cars that looked lived in and found none. After circling the parking lot twice, I headed to the hospital for my appointment. What could He have meant? I knew it was the Almighty's voice. As He had done these things frequently, but why was this happening now?

At the hospital, I continued looking for someone homeless, but none were on site. Feeling defeated, I decided to go inside and check-in for the appointment. When I was waiting for the receptionist to call me forward, I overheard her talking to someone on the phone she would figure out how to get some money. At once, I was flooded with the knowledge that she was the one I was supposed to give the $20! I was to tell her the Almighty heard her prayer—I was terrified! This woman was not who I expected to share His word. All my money was in the vehicle because I was about to do another MRI. How do I even approach her with this information?

The lady now called me forward to check-in, and I asked if everything was okay? She stated that she needed more money for child care if she was going to be able to keep working. My heart dropped, and as I was about to share with her what happened to me, she checked me in. Her questions led the conversation another way, and I needed to interrupt her. Also, her colleague was nearby, and I didn't want to embarrass her. Before I knew it, she was done and asked me to have a seat in the waiting room. What happened? Did I fear people more than the Almighty Himself? I prayed in the waiting room that if she indeed was the one, He wanted me to speak to; that He would give me another opportunity.

After my testing was complete, I was walking to the parking lot. The same lady was right there in the hallway talking with another employee. Here was my second chance to be obedient. I was so scared that I might embarrass her I decided to not say anything. She looked up and started talking to me, and I couldn't hear a word she said! I walked right past her, and tears fell from my face, and my walk increased until I made it to the van. Something profound was revealed that day; I feared what other people thought more than my obedience to His voice. I drove home, feeling defeated. So often I had done what He said, but He was raising the stakes now. He wanted me to be a vessel that would respond in any situation, even when it's uncomfortable or embarrassing.

A Family or Congregational Worship?

The moment we were in was a test of our faith. Would we continue to serve Him without an audience? Could our actions throughout each day truly show we believed in Him? We watched Sabbath services online and continued our studies at home. We seemed more relaxed now, and having everyone together during the day of rest was healing and comfortable. We grew even closer as a family. This comfort felt good, but I missed the people, and time of worship with the congregation. Being comfortable was not why I wanted to be home, but for obedience. I truly believed that the Almighty wanted me to teach and be with my family on the Sabbath.

For a few weeks now, the Almighty was pushing me to visit a congregation a few miles from our house. I didn't fully understand why there; I didn't agree with some of their theologies. But the calling to go wasn't going away, and the night before I went, I hardly slept. When I arrived, they were very friendly. Offered me snacks and drinks and directed me to an adult Bible study. They put me in the seniors' class that morning, which was very odd as I was only forty years old. This was my cue though, the Almighty was directing me to share something that morning. During the Bible study, the teacher asked many questions, and most sat there silent. I wanted them to respond at least once before answering. The Almighty was testing me again. Was I going to fear people or Him? I raised my hand and responded with accuracy and added to the situation with a question. This started some dialog that brought the class to life, and others shared real situations and even asking questions on how to deal with things. This was an awkward situation to be sharing with those I consider elders. Surprisingly, they were very receptive, and the Almighty spoke so much wisdom through me. All was received, and I felt relieved. After the class, the teacher and many of the students thanked me with sincerity. Was I done with my assignment? Could I go home now?

I stayed for the morning service. The praise and worship time felt like a rock concert. The lights were turned down low, and fog machines were going off, and the stage lights were flashing. The whole thing seemed so unreverent to the Almighty! At the end of the service, they had an altar call and invited anyone up who needed prayer. I knew I needed to go and publicly repent for I had ignored the Almighty's voice a few months before. This was another part of why I was there. I ignored His call with the receptionist at the hospital, and now He was using me again. I didn't want to fail at responding to His call!

The lead elder asked what I needed prayer for, and I shared that I wasn't listening fully to His voice and wanted more courage to not be scared. After we prayed, he asked if he could share with the congregation what I had said, I agreed. He told the people how we need to be vulnerable and open to change in our lives. He was thankful that a guest wasn't afraid to come forward and set an example for them to follow. I now knew why the Almighty wanted me there—to be an example. Even at my own expense of what little pride I had, He wanted to use me so He would be glorified. I was encouraged, and so were they; but ultimately, the Almighty was honored! This was also a powerful lesson on humility and obedience. I would not willingly attend a congregation like this, nor expose my family to their awkward behaviors. The unorthodox ways the Almighty used me that day increased my faith and understanding. My knowledge is not as crucial as my obedience. He humbled me so he could be glorified. I also learned how vital family worship is if we want our children to believe. First, we must start with ourselves, then our families, and then the congregations.

It was also becoming apparent that the scare from the dream a few months ago was not a physical danger, but a spiritual one. My daughter looked up to her mom and followed her actions. If my wife wasn't as excited about the Almighty's word, why would she be? Why should she take an interest in a book that sat on a shelf and collected dust? Instead of feeling defeated, I stayed focused on teaching the family and growing together in unity. I continued doing the nightly Bible stories and discussions with the whole family. During meals, I would share as much as I could of how the Almighty was teaching me things in my life.

After a few months of living in our 'cave,' I wanted to feel the outside breeze. In my spirit, I knew this was a season of growth, and we were growing together in the wilderness. The Feast of Tabernacles was coming up in the fall, and we wanted to celebrate with other Believers. The last year we camped out in my parents' back yard and attended a local congregation. Still, this year I tried to find a group of Believers who desired to dwell and fellowship together all week long. It was the only opportunity that stood promising the growth, nearness, and worship desired for our Creator. I searched for several weeks, but so many groups were commercialized. They were selling an experience where you show up and are taken care of throughout the week. No offense, but I wanted to have more responsibility for spending this time with my family, and we didn't need people cooking our meals.

I expressed my concerns to my wife, and we prayed about finding the right place, and a group of Believers to be with during these set-apart days. She decided to look online and see what she could find. I wasn't sure about it as I thought, "How is she going to find anything? I had been looking for days and not getting very far." Within a few seconds, she found a website and asked me what I thought. To my surprise, it was a legitimate group, better than anyone I had ever noticed before now. They were small, not looking for hundreds of dollars, but encouraging clean family fellowship. This group was the assembly we were supposed to meet with, and the Almighty used my wife to identify precisely where He wanted us to keep the feast that year.

When we first met up with the group, things were a little stressed. We were delayed a half-day and wanted all our work done and set up before the Sabbath started. To our surprise, the host family was running behind too. They were very welcoming and friendly people, and it was a joy to dwell with each other in unity. Many of the people there seemed very similar to us. They were very dedicated to the Almighty and doing their best to learn and do everything he tells us. We all worked together to help get set up, and the whole week was spent worshiping and growing closer to our Creator.

TAKE THE PLUNGE

Can anyone forbid water, that these should not be baptized who have received the Holy Spirit just as we have?' And he commanded them to be baptized in the name of the Lord. Then they asked him to stay a few days.

(Acts 10:47-48)

The week of celebration for The Feast of Tabernacles was such a blessing! My favorite part is the remembrance of how the Son of the Almighty came to Earth to Tabernacle with mankind; and how He will soon return. We praised and worshiped the Almighty and met many new friends. In the mornings, the men gathered around the campfire and talked about spiritually leading our families. I loved the amount of responsibility each man was taking for their households. The soberness of everyone was something I could now appreciate as I, too, loved being accountable for my loved ones. The maturity and diversity of the group was simply amazing.

There were many seasoned Believers there ranging in different ages and different walks on how they ended up to their current point. I wouldn't speak for everyone, but I believe most saw the church as a body of Believers, not a building, membership, or any form of headship. We are the leaders of our families and responsible for providing spiritual leadership. Our Head is the Son of the Almighty Himself.

Judging Versus Loving

This week was full of lessons, teachings, and a few experiences that changed my life. One lesson I got was our love for others is of the heart and not only appearances. The host family, and most people there, were pleasant and outgoing, but I realized that wasn't the case for everyone. Some people looked pleasant, but once they talked, I realized I was the guinea pig for their next 'sermon.' I would politely listen and look for a place to interject warmly. Some then realized I already understood many of the concepts they shared, and they would stop, while others would continue on until there was no time left. I took this experience as a chance to examine myself and realized I was looking into a mirror.

The arrogance I had in times past made me think about my own pride. When I was chasing my dog down the streets in pajamas; or how I had tried to 'educate' others as if I had the Almighty's word all figured out! It was as if I was looking in a mirror and seeing a reflection of my spiritual self. I didn't like what I saw either. I experienced this sort of judgment in other congregations. I would think, "This person doesn't know me," but this time, I realized what mattered was I needed to take a hard look at myself from the inside out. I may love the Almighty with all my humbled heart and salvaged soul and renewed mind, but I needed to work on loving my neighbor as myself.

Often, I wanted to share with loved ones or anyone who would listen, but it was likely that my speech was as sandpaper on their eardrums. The harshness in my voice and desire to want to 'teach' made me realize I, too, was guilty of this behavior.

However, I realized that I was assuming. Neither of us knew each other, and I kept thinking of a quote from Theodore Roosevelt, *"Nobody cares how much you know, till they know how much you care."* At one point in the week, the lead elder even used this same quote during one of his messages. I took this as a clear sign I need to heed these words. I needed to get to know others personally before I could determine where they were spiritually. I vowed to myself to be patient with them until we were familiar with each other.

This concept of not knowing one another before passing judgment wasn't an entirely new one to me.

During my time in the military, especially in training, everyone looked tough and motivated on the first day. Still, after a few days, you could see who was truly dedicated to the mission, and tough on the inside to endure till the end. People who looked tough were not always equipped with the desire and understanding they were part of something bigger than themselves. The ones who united and helped their buddies finish the training were the ones who not only completed the training, but excelled beyond their peers.

My father was also a military man, and he used to tell me, "You can tell a lot about a person in the first five minutes of talking to them…" This idea was proving to be true in this circumstance, also. I needed to 'clean the inside of my cup,' meaning I needed to look at myself first before I could effectively help others. I had done this often in my life now, but I needed to do this daily. I needed a deep clean first to ensure I could maintain some sort of purity in my thoughts, words, and actions. Indeed, being led by the Spirit and not the flesh.

Stay Humble and Focused

About the middle of the week, there was a scheduled canoeing trip down the Caddo River. The idea was exciting, but the reality was daunting. I had grown up along the Arkansas River and had gone down often;

every year, overconfident people died. So the thought of taking my children down with a large group of people I just met spiritually but knew little about physically, terrified me.

We started this three-hour journey with a bang. I spent the first fifteen minutes teaching the children how to turn and back paddle, and could have used a few more days instructing them. As soon as most of the group had gone ahead, we took our turn, negotiating each bend in the river. The first one, we needed a sharp left, and I directed the children accordingly. As the steep bank kept getting closer, I was in the rear, trying to turn the canoe. It seemed hopeless, and all I could do was tell the children to brace. Fortunately, I had taught them that command already. A few minutes later, a seasoned elder approached me and asked if I had ever done this before. Whatever pride I had was quickly deteriorated at this point. I let him know I had, but it had been a long time. He gave me some beneficial pointers that helped us the rest of the way. So losing my pride and gaining control was worth the exchange.

The primary lesson my children and I learned was we had to stay focused on where we wanted to go, not what we wanted to avoid. Sometimes we would get distracted by the surrounding beauty or an intimidating tree in the way. We had to also communicate with each other as many times as we were contradicting each other and would have to quickly correct. We made it through humbled and exhausted, but the experience itself brought us closer to each other and to the Almighty.

A Dream to Confirm My Baptism

As the Feast week progressed, some people got baptized, and I watched as they did. I had been baptized before, but so much had happened in the last few years. Also, there were several years where I had completely walked away from the faith in the Almighty, and wanted to rededicate my life to Him publicly. One of the nights, I cried out to Him and asked if I should do the baptism. I also asked Him if I was worthy and ready because there was a little doubt. The doubt was not in myself, but that when I had approached an elder earlier that week, he seemed very hesitant. Most likely because he didn't know me. I hoped he was just cautious, but the sting of him not seeing the apparent good in me really made me question what I looked like to others. Did my actions and speech not reflect who I had become on the inside? I was a person who did my best to glorify the Almighty in everything.

Once I fell asleep, I had the most remarkable dream of my whole life! I was there next to the Son of the Almighty, and He was filling me with light. This light was so powerful because it could shine through walls! Once I was full of His brightness, I had complete peace and full power but was not more powerful than the Almighty Himself. It was an outright remarkable moment where I was able to go up to people I knew and share this light, and they were instantly healed and whole! After waking up, you can imagine the letdown of reality from a dream like that. I immediately went to the Almighty in prayer and thanked Him for such an astonishing vision. I've had a lot of dreams in my lifetime. This one, however, was an answer to my prayer that night. I knew the Set-Apart Spirit already dwelled in me, but my flesh was still easily offended. I had to humble myself and continue on regardless of what others may have thought.

The next morning, I talked with one of the elders and asked if he would take some time to counsel me, and he agreed. What a relief it was to find someone who would take time and help disciple another, even when it was inconvenient. This selfless act was much appreciated, and the guidance he gave me helped shape who I've become today. I knew this time given to me needed to be paid forward in the future.

Discipleship, bringing others to be baptized, and making disciples was a commandment from the Son of the Almighty. For some reason, this was missing in my walk. I was learning and teaching my family, but I needed to be baptized. There was a six-year gap where I had completely fallen away from the Almighty and was in the world. I felt a lot like Cornelius because I knew I had received the Set-Apart Spirit in my life over eighteen months prior, and I wanted to go all the way. Too much change in our lives proved the power of the Almighty at work.

I needed to die on the inside entirely and outwardly show it. I had to change my thinking and stop making excuses and agree to sin no more. As the Son of the Almighty forgave Believers, He told them to sin no more after they were healed, not to return to their evil ways. I was one step closer now to overcoming, by outwardly demonstrating to my family what was changing on the inside. The next day I was baptized and was never the same.

TWO YEARS OF DEDICATION AND LEARNING

But this is the covenant that I will make with the house of Israel after those days, says the LORD: I will put My law in their minds, and write it on their hearts; and I will be their God, and they shall be My people.

(Jeremiah 31:33)

The baptism marked a new beginning in time for me. I had outwardly showed my commitment to the Almighty in front of my family, and it made a huge difference. Some struggles with my flesh battling with the Spirit were now resolved. I was experiencing more self-control than ever before and becoming a solid example for my family. Jacqueline had developed a desire to read her Bible now and was becoming a lot more involved during family Bible studies. My son, Timothy, wanted even more time to study, so we got up at 5:30 every morning, and had personal reading time followed by prayer. At breakfast, we shared what we read that morning, and this simple daily commitment made an exponential difference in our growth and understanding of the Word of the Almighty. We even read and studied the Bible together on the Sabbath.

A few weeks had passed, and Jacqueline was informed that a relative had recently lost her husband. She lived in an apartment in Chicago and worked as a school teacher. Her loss was hard for her, and we felt so privileged to be able to be there for her. I don't know how much help we were, but we were able to share some tears and scriptures. I hadn't cried like that since we lost William, and it was as if the Almighty was allowing me to feel her physical and emotional pain. Her heart felt like it was being stabbed and bleeding out her "other half." We shared many meals and laughed together. Watching her go through each item in the house, and hearing the story behind these articles helped me realize our primary purpose was to be there and let her talk, and heal. This time was very similar to other assignments the Almighty had given us; we tried to be a blessing to others and received a bigger blessing.

At the end of our visit, we attended her congregation. There, she was actively involved and a great pianist. The songs were so anointed, and I can still hear them! "Vic-tor-y is mine! Vic-tor-y is mine! Vic-tor-y to-day is mine..." What a joy it was to praise the

Almighty together! Her husband was a professional photographer and had donated his talents and time to make a giant collage on one of the walls. On the wall were the families and members of the congregation. Some photos showed people working in the community garden, laughing with brothers and sisters, and praising the Almighty.

Many members of the congregation kept asking us if we were enjoying our time in Chicago. They wanted to know where we visited and what we did. We came to be with family and grieve, not a vacation. Our entire mission was to be used by the Almighty to show love to our family. We wanted our extended family to know that even though we are far away that we care.

Before heading back to her apartment and saying goodbye, she wanted to drop off some things to donate for those less fortunate. She took us on tour through some historic sites that were very poverty-stricken. I felt so privileged to be with her and hear all the challenges she had witnessed over the decades. Along the way, she asked me a question I will never forget. She wanted my opinion on how I felt about a female homosexual pastor teaching the congregation. Fortunately, I had been humbled by the Almighty for this moment and was able to respond with love. I had already experienced that my opinions mean very little. What the Almighty wanted me to do was show love to my neighbor. He is the judge, and His Word tells us what is right. His Word cuts right through confusion and provides clarity in any circumstance.

The Almighty was also tugging at my heart to spend more time in prayer. I prayed several times throughout the day, but it seemed He wanted more. It was time to humble myself a little more and bend the knee to show full submission to my King. I dedicated some time just before going to bed. What I thought might be a few extra minutes was turning into long periods that were going by quickly. I discovered prayer was needed for my brothers and sisters in the faith— also, the leaders, both spiritual and governmental. Extended family members and friends of the past needed to be remembered, thought of, and prayed for. Even past enemies and those who had wronged me were becoming part of my daily time with the Almighty. He loves everyone and wants to see us all come to know and love His ways.

We Returned to the Former Congregation

About four months later marked the second anniversary since I had committed my life to the Almighty. We were still considering moving to a smaller house with more land and had found a few promising properties in Texas. Before putting an offer on one, I decided to pray and see if this was the Almighty's will. That night I had a dream I was back at the congregation we had stepped away from and missed so much. When I woke up, I asked the Almighty if this was from Him and what it meant. Still, before I could even finish praying, I was flooded with the knowledge to go back to the former congregation and learn—such a humbling experience. I thought we were no longer going to attend this congregation because of the previous dream I had and had already stepped away because we felt unsafe. But now, a fantastic realization came; we were stepping away to grow as a family, but it was now time to go back. I didn't fully understand why this was happening, but the desire to move became unimportant. We had received new orders from the Almighty Himself to stay put and learn some more.

I emailed the lead elder of the congregation and asked if it would be okay for our family to visit. He responded with, "Of course, you are welcome." I didn't have to ask, but I respect him and the congregation. I needed to hear, "You are welcome" because it gave me confirmation. The fear we used to have was overruled by the Almighty. He said, "Go and learn." so we went back. We were back at the congregation for a few weeks and believed the Almighty wanted us to be there for a while.

The Almighty Our Source and Peace

A few weeks later, there was a worldwide pandemic from a virus called coronavirus or COVID-19. This virus had caused the entire country to go to a near shutdown. Schools had been closed. Places of worship had been closed. Even the congregation we had attended the last three Sabbaths had been closed, but continued to share in an online environment. Many of the stores, restaurants, and businesses had slowed down or changed to curbside pickup. My heart went out to those who were hurting and hoped they found great comfort in the Source. As real as this virus was, the peace I had during the event was comforting. I genuinely believed the Almighty was protecting us from fear and sickness. Still, even if we were to get sick or die, my faith in the resurrection brought tremendous comfort.

This period in life was an excellent opportunity to shine out the light in us—to radiate the brightness we have in our lives by the Word. It was also a time we could see that the last two years of obedience had paid off. Our school was still opened and running at full speed. Our congregating as a family to worship the Almighty was already in place and performed daily. Our storehouses were stocked and continued to be filled. Our simple lifestyle allowed us to give more to others than ever before. We were growing in understanding and sharing. With all of these tangible miracles amid a devouring pandemic, even if we didn't have this peace, we would continue to praise the Almighty. He makes life unique, and worth living!

The Almighty protected us from making a dangerous move. He already knew the Coronavirus was coming before we did. Downsizing our home once seemed like a good plan, but I trusted Him when He said to stay put. I didn't fully understand why at the time, but with the global pandemic at hand, I could see it was wise to be settled and safe at our Oklahoma home for the time being. I had learned that it is essential to go to Him in prayer before making any decision, and when He answers to be obedient. What seemed like a good idea a month before would have been a considerable hardship on my family during those months where people had many restrictions. It was also essential I gave Him the praise and glory because He brought and kept my family together.

My Transformation

Looking out the window of our home in Oklahoma, I saw a beautiful sunset, marking the end of another day worshiping the Almighty. This time of great peace created a desire in me to share my testimony with all who will listen.

Never did I think that during my times of selfishness, I would enjoy being a husband and a father along with the constant physical pain and fatigue I often felt. I certainly never thought that with all this, I would be the happiest and most at peace in my life thus far. It's only because of the Almighty, and because I'm weak, it gives Him all the glory. I've already proved I couldn't do life lovingly on my own. He hasn't taken away all my sickness yet, but in many ways, He already has.

This is my story of how the Almighty has been real and worked in my life. How at times I had turned to my desires and missed out on the blessings and favor, while at other times I obeyed the Almighty, turned to Him, and received His complete peace. There were many habits, traditions, and things in my life I gave up because I realized it went against the Almighty's word. Once I stopped idolizing myself and began worshipping Him, it was so easy to change and leave the ways of the world. It was easy to have a real relationship with the Almighty!

The Almighty gave me His Son as an example to follow, and any time I'm not sure how to deal with something, I can look to Him for guidance. If something seems too big, I remind myself that greater is He that dwells inside me than any obstacle I might be facing.

The Almighty's amazing grace has brought me into freedom and mercy, to obey His instructions to the best of my abilities, and continue this process of sanctification and growth. I realize how difficult it is to be like the Son of the Almighty in my words and works, but I love trying. I believe that He wants me to be busy growing, sharing, and teaching others of His story through love and living as an example. I also realize this is a process, and I have not yet made it into His kingdom—I have much to learn. I must be humble and serve Him and others.

The Almighty wants me to be willing to give up anyone, or anything, I love just as he did. Love is a sacrifice to the Almighty and our neighbor. I also realized that when I think I've arrived, there is yet another task at hand. Recognizing that I have fallen short of the glory of the Almighty. I must go to Him daily in prayer, be washed in His pure Word, and do whatever He asks of me every day. There is a process after the transformation, and His grace helps achieve miracles in my life. He is the Almighty. There isn't anything too challenging for Him—the Mighty One of Abraham, Isaac, and Jacob. I follow His Son for my standard, and with the help from the Set-Apart Spirit, I can do all things according to His will!

CLOSING THOUGHTS

L et us hear the conclusion of the whole matter: Fear God and keep His commandments, For this is man's all.

(Ecclesiastes 12:13)

With so much transformation in my life, I was given a strong desire to share my story. As several destructive addictions and habits heap our world today, I believe my testimony of how I overcame will arouse the faith in you. As you find the Almighty to set you free with a great deliverance! So many faithful servants of the Almighty have shared and encouraged me, which allowed me to grow. Now, it's my turn to step up and share with the world how He is delivering me.

So these decades of searching for the truth, running from responsibility, and learning to live more humbly, can be summed up with the following: I'm still a work in progress. The problems we have today do not differ from when the Son of the Almighty walked here on earth. They do not differ from when Moses, Abraham, and Adam lived either. We are not the Almighty, and we are not in charge. When we think we are, that's when selfishness, disappointment, guilt, anger, jealousy, and all other sins exist. It's our choices in whom we will serve each moment. It's our time and energy that gets our true votes, and shows who, or what, we truly worship. Each day we must choose whom we will serve. Are we listening to the words of the Almighty?

I grew up in a church, read and studied the Bible often, but what I had was religion, not a relationship. I had a false covering, not a commitment. I compared myself to those that were doing worse than me to confirm I was doing well. Rather than comparing myself to the Son of the Almighty and seeing I fell short. It wasn't a daily walk that kept me focused on the Priority of living, but was mixed with the world and my desires. Why else were we created but to have a relationship that glorifies the Almighty Himself? We were not intended to break into sects when disagreements arise!

Ever wonder why someone doesn't believe the same? It's because we did not speak their language, and we can only do that when we let the Almighty come in, do the work, and get all the glory! We can break down those walls amongst Believers with the words of the Almighty. Let us love the Almighty with all our heart, with all our soul, and with all our might. We are to love our neighbor as ourselves. When someone is hurting, we are to help them and show the Almighty's love. Not with so much our words, but with our actions. Let it not be ignored that we are responsible for the ones we are with, to love them.

When I became a sincere Believer, I became an honest doer; and nothing, nor anyone, could shut me up nor stop me from loving the Almighty. The good works of the Almighty that started inside me spread to my children and eventually to my wife. I believe it is next spreading to the congregation and beyond. If we want our family to have a relationship with the Creator, then we must spend time with them and worship the Almighty together. Not on certain days of the week with a congregation, but praise Him when we first wake up on our own. Ask Him if He spoke to us in our sleep. Speak to Him throughout the day and bless and praise Him for everything He has given us, even the things we don't realize He's given us. Take time daily to meet as a family and worship Him. Get to know Him in His Word so we can recognize and do what He desires of us.

When we are tired at the end of the day, bless Him and pray for those whom we love, pray for those who rule over us, and pray for those who hurt us. Take time throughout the day to get to know Him through His Word and His faithful servants. Do not let the sun go down when we have someone to forgive, or to repent to. Once that's done, go to our Father in Heaven and offer Him praise for the peace He's given us. Then pray for the entire body of Believers, pray for those searching for the Anointed One to find Him, and that the scales will fall from their eyes. So the truth will be revealed to them. Thank the Son of the Almighty for ascending to Our Father in Heaven as a perfect person who dropped His blood in the tabernacle, not made by man. And then, we will have greater peace.

The Almighty wants to tear down the walls of our hearts and minds, our understandings, and comfort zones. We cannot put Him in a building, nor a religion. He wants us to look past the teachings and traditions to see He is in charge, and desires our obedience and love. Let us continue to share our testimonies of the Almighty in truth and sincerity.

I hope this book has inspired you to draw closer to the Almighty. To look past the challenges and see we truly can overcome anything, whatever it may be. As long as we are willing to realize we are responsible for the sins in our lives, and accepting the covering of the Lamb. Following Him, not with a spirit of the flesh, but the Set-Apart Spirit of hope and righteousness.

Our battles are not against flesh and blood. Look at how we all have been deceived a little at a time. We need to gain back the truth and righteousness until we have finished the race. All of us should be listening to the Good Shepherd and follow Him—not being swayed the directions of the world. If we are counting solely on any spiritual leader other than Him, we need to work towards independence from them and look to the Prince of Peace. Comparing ourselves to His righteousness, not others.

For the seasoned Believer, I want to challenge you to remember that none of us are above the lurking deceptions of this world. Stay close to—and hungry for—the Truth. Please do not think you are above these spiritual attacks. Salvation is a gift, and so is our free will. I exhort you to give back to Him that gift with righteousness! Our lives should shine with freedom from sins and be light in the darkness. Stay close to the Almighty in spirit and in truth.

I'm humbled and honored to take a moment to raise awareness for mental health, as it is something I have struggled with for over a decade. I also want to raise awareness of our United States Veterans. Many have taken their own lives because of this heaviness of just trying to live. The sickness is hidden from the untrained eye, but the challenge to perform is so cumbersome. Many Veterans are too proud to get help. I know this because that was me. I was "self-medicating" to ease the pains invisible to others. Many issues were so vivid and gruesome that I purposefully left them out of this book. I could have easily been like the many fellow Soldiers, homeless, unable to hold a job, or be with families struggling in our streets today. Most people did not even know I was struggling. Without the Almighty in my life, I could not be able to love others the way I do today.

I hope this snapshot of my life refreshes us into appreciating the goodness given to all by the Creator Himself. Our most valuable assets are not ourselves or the things He has given us, but instead the relationships He has surrounded us with. A genuine connection with Him is so contagious that it spreads to all those along our path. Allowing Him into our lives can, and will, move mountains!

Thank you for reading my testimony. If you know someone who could use encouragement, please pass this book on.

SHARE YOUR TESTIMONY

I thought it good to declare the signs and wonders that the Most High God has worked for me.

(Daniel 4:2)